An AMA Research Study

DRUG ABUSE

The Workplace Issues

WITHDRAWN

AMA Membership Publications Division
American Management Association

This publication has been prepared by the AMA Membership Publications Division staff:

Don L. Bohl   Managing Editor
Eric Rolfe Greenberg   Research Project Director
Anne Skagen   Associate Editor
Yvette DeBow   Staff Writer

Dr. Dale Masi served as consultant in the design of the study and interpretation of questionnaire results, in addition to providing other valuable advice and direction.

Names of products or services provided herein are included to illustrate the types of such products and services available. No endorsement is intended or implied.

For information on the purchase of additional copies, see inside back cover.

Library of Congress Cataloging-in-Publication Data

Drug abuse, the workplace issues

    (AMA research study)
    1. Drugs and employment—United States.   2. Drugs—
Analysis.   3. Urine—Analysis.   I. American Management
Association.   AMA Membership Publications Division.
HF5549.5.D7D7   1987   658.3′822   86-32254
ISBN 0-8144-3511-4

This Research Study has been distributed to all members enrolled in the Human Resources Division of the American Management Association.

First Printing

Contents

Introduction

Weed. Dust. Horse. Juice.
Crack and *smack* and *snow* and *blow.*

These simple monosyllables pack immense emotional power today. In the welter of warnings and dire statistics, with such emotion-laden words sounding as a drumbeat, it's hard to keep in mind some simple facts:

Only a small percentage of American workers are true drug abusers. Most American workers are not regular users of illegal substances of any sort. Most who have experimented with illegal drugs at one time or another are not addicts and never will be, by any definition.

And yet drug abuse is certainly and legitimately a workplace issue. Drug usage has an immediate and ongoing impact on worker productivity, and thus on organizational performance and profit. Moreover, dealing with drug users and abusers tests the depth of a company's commitment to its workforce. "If you really do think of your employees as a 'human resource,'" an HR director told an AMA researcher, "then you have an obligation to help them through an employee assistance program. Otherwise, it's all just talk."

Do Numbers Define the Problem?

A rush of 1986 statistics on drug abuse produced occasional lapses in precision. Three to five million Americans have tried cocaine once, said the National Institute on Drug Abuse—a figure other researchers took to mean *regular* users. The Research Triangle Institute was frequently citied as the source of the estimated cost of drug abuse: $100 billion annually in lost worker productivity. But the RTI put this forward to cover the combined loss due to alcohol *and* drug abuse—and defined "lost productivity" as *lost worker earning power,* not industrial cost.

There is no clear line between use and abuse, and no way to count the number of true abusers. Experts gave AMA figures ranging from 2 to 5 percent of the American workforce. Alcoholism is believed to be a far more pervasive problem, placed as high as 10 percent.

According to Lee Dogoloff of the American Council for Drug Education, education and awareness programs are effective exactly because most substance *users* are not *addicts* with a physical dependency. Addicts must be detoxified; the occasional user may be educated.

Whatever the actual numbers, the most important statistic is a single digit: one. One job-impaired worker can create a problem of the greatest urgency. And human resources professionals with whom AMA talked insist that one-on-one intervention by a skilled counselor is most effective in dealing with workplace drug abuse.

Inevitably, managers dealing with the workplace issues of drug abuse must make a decision on whether or not current and/or prospective employees should be tested for drugs. Because of this, the separate and distinct questions of dealing with drug abusers and testing for drugs are often intertwined, and the benefits and problems which derive from either practice become hopelessly confused.

"I'm concerned about the amount of attention given to drug testing right now," said a medical director for a *Fortune* 100 steelmaker. "We're not going to solve the problem by testing everyone. Testing is getting too much attention, to the exclusion of other aspects of dealing with drug abuse."

Does this respondent's company test for drugs? Indeed it does. It began preemployment screening in 1977, and within the past year, hiring at a new site, it rejected *40 percent* of all job applicants after drug traces were found in urine samples. Without such screening, many of these applicants would have gone onto the payroll, with obvious implications for performance and safety.

Yet as of January 1987, only half of America's hundred largest industrial firms screen job applicants for drugs, and just 21.7 percent of the 1,090 firms responding to AMA's questionnaire have any drug testing program in place. A significant number have studied the issue and opted not to test—among them another *Fortune* 100 manufacturer, whose medical director told us what lay behind the decision.

"There are many variables to consider," he said. "Community problems. Plant security. What other companies in the area are doing. We considered these variables and others, and we haven't felt the need to test.

"This presupposes an active alcohol and substance abuse program in place, with good education of supervisors and co-workers as to the danger of drug abuse and how to spot job impairment. If you have that, there's no need to test."

There are, one may say, three layers to the controversy surrounding testing. At one level are such issues as accuracy, privacy, and legality. Most of these are capable of solution. If gas chromatography is used to validate all positive immunoassay tests, accuracy is really no longer an issue (cost may be). The privacy issue must be dealt with in the wider context of employee morale. Legal issues will yield to court decisions.

A second layer of controversy relates to the discrepancy between the tool and the solution. From a manager's point of view, the issue properly begins with job impairment—a problem that might stem from any number of sources: marital discord, financial woes, chronic depression, or a good case of the flu. (The sneezing and runny nose of the latter, by the way, might look like cocaine addition to an overly suspicious person.) The amount of attention thrown onto drug abuse may create tunnel vision. "If your only tool is a hammer," the old saying goes, "everything looks like a nail." With only a drug testing kit in the tool case, all performance problems may lead to a drug test—and a positive finding in itself may discover a symptom rather than a cause. If a worker is getting high to escape anxiety over a failing marriage, some companies may see effective employee assistance as going beyond the "drug problem" to address the reason behind it.

The third layer runs to public and private morality. Possession of an illegal substance is a criminal act—a low-level misdemeanor in some localities, a felony in others. Some employers may see drug testing as a tool to identify criminal activity among employees. Others, with equal force, may object to doing the sheriff's work for him—and wonder what to do if just such evidence comes to light.

Is drug testing an effective tool for confronting drug-related job impairment? Many of our respondents think it is, and cite statistics to back their claim. Others reject the idea in no uncertain terms, arguing that no amount of testing will ever ensure that an employee is mentally, physically and emotionally fit to do a job *on a given day*. "Why not have an air-traffic controller play a game of PacMan before he goes on duty?" asked one of our respondents. "If he gets to the second or third screen, he's fit to go to work. And that's going to tell you much more than a drug test taken six months before."

Preemployment screening—by far the most widespread drug testing practice among AMA respondents large and small—has its own limitations. Essentially, what one is testing is the applicant's discipline and intelligence. As will be seen, traces of cocaine leave the bloodstream within 48 hours of use; marijuana lingers far longer, as much as a month, but eventually disappears as well. Therefore, a negative finding may tell an employer only that an applicant has the "smarts and straights" to stay off coke for 2 days and off smoke for 30. Moreover, a positive finding for cocaine may result from the use of a codeine-based cold remedy.

For-cause testing—by far the most widespread practice applied to current employees—has its limitations as well. A supervisor needs good reason for initiating actions leading to testing, and the circumstances constituting "just cause" or "reasonable suspicion" are often difficult to define.

ABOUT THIS STUDY

These questions and concerns, reflecting awareness of substance abuse as a management issue, prompted the current AMA study.

We began in October 1986 by mailing 10,000 questionnaires to human resources directors on AMA membership lists and on the subscription list of our leading human resources publication, *Personnel*. Our selection was controlled to draw a representative sample of companies nationwide. The questionnaire emphasized that the company's response was important to our database, regardless of the action it had (or had not) taken on substance abuse. By our November cutoff date, we had received 1,090 usable responses for our tabulations.

At the same time, we telephoned the corporate headquarters of each of the hundred largest industrial companies in America. To ensure a candid response, we told all respondents that our report would not quote them by name nor identify their firms. Then we asked: what is your corporate policy regarding substance abuse? Your stance on preemployment screening, testing for cause, or periodic checks on current employees? If you test, what prompted program implementation, and how are you measuring its effectiveness? What are your concerns regarding test accuracy?

A third wave of research, more journalistic than systematic, focused on other issues: the importance of employee assistance programs (EAPs) in dealing with substance abuse, and the cost and effectiveness of treatment methods.

Several important findings emerged from this investigation:

- "Smart supervisors" (people who know how to spot possible impairment and intervene), backed by an aggressive program aimed at stopping abuse and providing rehabilitation, are by far the most important agents in the drive for a drug-free workplace. Voiced repeatedly during the in-depth interviews, this assessment draws dramatic significance from the incidence-of-referral data provided by more than 500 respondents. *Among companies engaged in drug testing, the number of rehabilitative referrals triples if a training and educational initiative is part of the firm's attack on drug abuse.* Among companies not testing, the referral rate is more than double if an educational initiative is present.
- Companies that test for abuse are more likely to offer help to the employees in trouble, to educate their workforce on the dangers of worksite drug use, and to train managers and supervisors in how to approach possible impairment.

About half the companies now engaged in drug testing have such educational programs in place, compared with only about 20 percent of those that do not. The higher incidence within the former group is easily explained. The concerns that led to testing prompted a basic question: Is the program to be punitive, or rehabilitative? If the latter was the guiding objective, then something far broader than testing would be needed.

These findings will come as no surprise to those firms with rehabilitative and educational programs in place. For organizations that have yet to confront the problem on the level of "smart supervisors," these insights have far-reaching significance.

Among our other findings, primarily the questionnaire data:

- Significant numbers of firms in the service sector have considered, then rejected the idea of testing. The less pressing the issues of workplace or public safety, the greater the difficulty in formulating a clear rationale and cost-justification for testing. Other techniques—a firm policy, a clear management stand, and (again) education and training—are considered equal in result and far more cost-effective.

- Nevertheless, there has been a rapid increase in the number of companies testing, and the trend will continue into 1987. Late in 1985, the U.S. Drug Enforcement Administration estimated that about 25 percent of the *Fortune* 500 companies were testing. Our interviews reveal that about half of the *Fortune* 100 firms are doing some kind of preemployment testing at one or more sites, and testing for cause at most sites.

- Smaller firms are following the lead, but at a lesser pace. Among respondents with less than $500 million in annual sales, about 20 percent are testing, and of those, nine out of ten began in 1985 and 1986. Very few have stepped into the controversial arena of random and periodic testing.

- Almost half of the respondents whose firms are testing feel uncertain about the efficacy of this tool. For preemployment screening, respondents gauge impact in terms of problem avoidance and deterrence. Applied to current employees, testing is not a solution, say the respondents. It's one tool to help identify a problem.

- Although 9 percent of respondent firms see drug abuse as an automatic ticket to the unemployment line, two-thirds see assistance and rehabilitation as the most appropriate response.

Finally, several conclusions based on interviews with a variety of professional consultants active in areas related to drug abuse:

- There are currently few restrictions on a private-sector employer's decision to test for drug use. *But testing of every sort is under court challenge.* Every decision rendered to date has held that random testing of *public* employees is an "unreasonable search" and therefore a violation of constitutional guarantees. The law regarding preemployment screening, and any type of testing of private sector employees, is less certain. The application of various federal hiring laws is in dispute.
- Employee assistance programs are striving for ways to help their organizations rehabilitate drug abusers, but many EAPs are unproven in this area. Longstanding techniques to deal with alcohol abusers do not necessarily apply in this new field.
- Cost of treatment for drug abuse is beginning to become an important issue. Although alternatives to conventional hospital treatment are less costly, these avenues raise controversy in many circles.

AMA has gone to the experts for opinions in the respective fields of law, employee assistance, and test technology. Loren Siegel, an attorney who has monitored litigation and arbitration in this arena for some time, summarizes the legal issues in Chapter 2. Because of her association with the American Civil Liberties Union, Ms. Siegel is in a excellent position to identify those trends that may lead to curtailment of some testing practices. Dr. Dale Masi, whose name is synonymous with employee assistance, comments on EAPs and their difficulties in dealing with substance abuse in Chapter 4. Abbott Laboratories contributes an explication of testing methods in Appendix II.

Senior managers, human resources directors, medical officers, and employee relations experts may be forgiven if they feel caught in a stampede. The media plays the story on page one, the marketers ride the wave; even the President and Mrs. Reagan appear on prime-time television to urge an end to the "drug plague." But the search for solutions must take place against a background of understanding. The dimensions and complexities of workplace drug abuse do not yield to easy answers. Nearly half of the companies we surveyed have yet to shape their corporate policies on drug abuse. Of those that have a policy in place, most seem to be managing their programs in a humane, responsible, and carefully thought out manner. However, our survey results do point to a significant minority of companies that appear to be turning a deaf ear to sound legal and pharmaceutical advice, and to recent management experience. *Drug Abuse: The Workplace Issues* is offered as a guide to all.

1

The AMA Survey on Approaches to Workplace Drug Abuse

MOST OF the 1,090 companies responding to AMA's questionnaire—a shade under 80 percent—reported that they do no drug testing at present. But few have made a final decision against testing. As Exhibit 1.1 shows, just 8.6 percent replied that they have studied and rejected the idea.

Those 94 companies gave us definite reasons for deciding against testing. Half feared a negative impact on employee morale. Nearly two-thirds doubted the accuracy of test results, and 40 percent thought that testing, even if accurate, would not necessarily indicate job impairment. For one respondent in four, costs were a factor in the turn against testing.

But the reason most frequently cited was the moral/legal issue—the invasion of employee privacy. Regardless of corporate size or worksite population, guarding the rights of the individual counted highest among reasons why 94 firms considered, then rejected the idea of drug testing. And despite the exigencies of worksite safety, a higher percentage (74 percent) of manufacturing companies cited the privacy issue than service companies (67 percent).

Exhibit 1.1. Where companies stand on the testing issue.

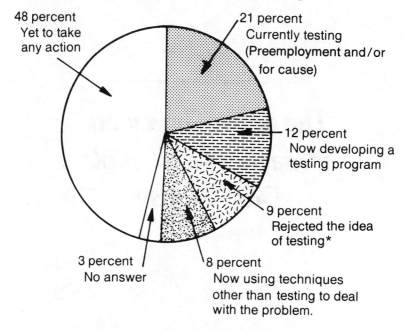

48 percent
Yet to take
any action

21 percent
Currently testing
(Preemployment and/or
for cause)

12 percent
Now developing a
testing program

9 percent
Rejected the idea
of testing*

3 percent
No answer

8 percent
Now using techniques
other than testing to deal
with the problem.

*Reasons for rejecting (percent):
- --68 Moral issues/invasion of privacy
- --63 Inaccuracy
- --53 Negative impact on morale
- --43 Positive test shows use, not abuse or impairment
- --28 Cost
- --17 Management opposition
- --16 Employee opposition
- -- 7 Union opposition

Notes: N = 1,090 Because respondents could check more than
one reason for rejecting testing, total exceeds 100.

CASE IN POINT

"It costs us at least $25,000 to hire and train an average employee,"
states Lewis Maltby, vice president of Drexelbrook Controls Inc., a

Horsham, Pennsylvania, manufacturer of precision instruments. "And it would be absurd to think about firing an employee on the basis of a test that isn't much better than flipping a coin."

Like many respondents who have come down against testing, Maltby has done so for more than one reason. Accuracy is one obstacle, the inability of a test to show impairment, another. But unlike many of our respondents, employee morale weighed heaviest in this case.

"We want every employee to give us a 100 percent effort every day. By and large, we get it. But that kind of commitment doesn't come easily. You have to earn it. One way to earn it is to treat employees like adults.

"But drug testing flies in the face of all that. Instead of trusting our employees to come to work physically and mentally prepared, we would be treating them like sneaky children who have to be watched constantly."

Maltby's alternative to testing is what he calls "good people management." This involves, first of all, rigorous checks on all job candidates, even "floor sweepers." Questions about a candidate's past work record (quality of work, absenteeism, etc.) are put to the candidate's former supervisor, not to the personnel department. Second, "people management" means getting to know employees personally. If the worker has a home problem that's spilling over into work, the company is willing to help. (Maltby notes that he has helped employees cope with problems ranging from financial needs to landlord disputes.) Third, it means telling employees what performance is expected—and mandating that supervisors sit down and discuss problems when performance falls short.

The approach works, as far as Maltby and the company are concerned. Yes, the firm has had one problem with an employee who was using drugs. And yes, the supervisor did spot the problem, and the employee accepted the offer for help.

THE OVERALL PICTURE

Two companies in ten test in some manner, and nearly one in ten has studied and rejected the idea. Of the rest, 12 percent are in the process of developing a drug testing program, and 8 percent are content to use techniques other than testing to identify drug abusers. Of the entire

Exhibit 1.2. Use of surveillance techniques.

Surveillance techniques	Companies not testing	Companies testing
Are you using any types of surveillance techniques?		
Yes	12%	26%
No	88	74
Which techniques?		
— checking lunchboxes and lockers	3%	12%
— undercover agents	4	10
— dogs	1	2
— other	7	3

Note: Respondents were allowed to check more than one type of surveillance technique, if applicable.

AMA sample, almost half—48 percent—said that they had yet to take any stance on the issue of testing, and 3 percent made no answer to the question—passive response, then, from half our sample on the issue of drug testing.

But these firms are far from passive on the issue of drug *abuse*. An overwhelming 93.5 percent reported dealing with cases of drug abuse in 1986. And most are dealing with the problem without resort to testing. Of the 856 non-testers, 26 percent have promulgated a corporate policy on drug abuse, and 24 percent report that a policy is currently in development.

Companies that do no testing must turn to other means of spotting drug abusers. But (as Exhibit 1.2 shows) drastic measures are not a popular alternative. Just 4 percent of non-testing companies use undercover agents among the workforce to ferret out pushers or users. Only 3 percent conduct searches of employees or workspaces. A mere 1 percent use dogs to sniff out offenders.

But with the decision to test, there occurs a concomitant rise in other search procedures. Companies that test are twice as likely to use dogs, more than twice as likely to use undercover agents, and nearly five times more likely to check lunchboxes, employee lockers, or other locations where drugs might be discovered.

What are the elements of a policy that excludes testing? By and large, such a policy must depend on supervisors to spot job impairment and refer the employee to the appropriate company resource. But while half the firms that test have also implemented a formal program to educate managers or workers on the signs of drug abuse or its dangers to self and co-workers, only one in five of the non-testing companies have done so. These firms are prime targets for the educational materials rushing onto the market to serve this very need. AMA's review of these products appears in Chapter 3.

And if, by whatever means, an employee is identified as a substance abuser? Very few of our respondents—just 8 percent—automatically discharge the offender. By far the most common policy is referral to an appropriate resource. The larger the company, the more likely it is to have an in-house employee assistance program (EAP) in place; our sample showed that large companies—those with more than $500 million in annual sales—were twice as likely to refer abusers to an EAP as were smaller companies, with sales under $50 million (see Exhibit 1.3).

Exhibit 1.3. Percentage of respondents handling substance-abuse referrals through an employee assistance program (EAP).

Annual sales or budget	Companies not testing for drug abuse		Companies currently testing for drug abuse	
	In-house EAP	Consortium EAP	In-house EAP	Consortium EAP
Under $50 million	14%	8%	24%	4%
$50-$499 million	27	12	28	14
$500 million or more	32	19	48	8
Total sample	20	11	31	10

Some of the mid-sized and smaller firms, as well as a significant number of the large ones—19 percent—had recourse to a consortium or network EAP. Others turned the problem over to a company physician or medical deparment. But in every instance, the companies with formal testing practices were more likely to employ rehabilitative services than were non-testing firms.

In total, two-thirds of the AMA sample were willing to give rehabilitative services a chance. The rest—less the 8 percent who fire the offender immediately—devise probationary periods, special supervision, official warnings placed in personnel files, and other such cautionary measures.

Unhappily, EAPs are not universally prepared to deal with drug offenders. As we report in Chapter 4, the methods that have proven effective in years of treating alcohol abusers are not necessarily successful in this newer field of substance abuse. Here again, new products and services are coming onto the market to fill the void.

In the ultimate, the drug abuser who refuses rehabilitation or who cannot kick the habit must go. Half of the companies that test for drugs have fired an employee for drug-related job impairment or illegal activity. Only 26 percent of the non-testing companies have done so. Here as elsewhere—in education programs, rehabilitative services, and search methods other than testing—the respondents who have inaugurated drug-testing procedures have an edge in dealing with drug abuse at work.

The reason? Not that they test, but that in devising a testing policy, they have addressed the other issues that surround the problem. AMA's findings echo the opinion voiced in many of our research interviews: that testing in itself is not the answer, but just one support in an overarching policy to attack workplace substance abuse.

PROFILES OF COMPANIES NOW TESTING

The motivation is written in large, red letters: DANGER.

"If we were making razor blades or underwear, it would be a different story," a major oil company told our researchers. "But those refineries are high-temperature, high-pressure places, and we gotta watch out for the safety of our men. Our policy is simple: you got a problem, either you get it fixed or you get the hell out."

For an equally colorful statement, here's how the manager of one of the largest warehousing operations in the U.S. put it. "Picture one of those warehouses—40 aisles, each aisle 40 feet high—a fork lift in each aisle and automatic conveyor machinery that takes material to the ceiling. That machiney can bite off arms and legs without stopping. Now, say that 10 percent of the men are high on something—or hungover from being on something the night before. . . . it's a chance we just can't afford to take."

PREEMPLOYMENT AND CURRENT-EMPLOYEE TESTING

Of the 234 companies with testing programs in place—

- 92 percent do preemployment testing
- 77 percent do some kind of testing of current employees, for-cause being pervasive.
- Only 12 percent do periodic testing (for example, as part of an annual physical examination), and 8 percent do random testing.

Consequently, discussion of testing programs in this section refers predominately to preemployment and for-cause programs.

Other motivations for screening range from the need to correct problems ("We had reports people were selling stuff in the plant") to personal vendettas to purge social ills ("Drug abuse is a sickness in our society. If enough companies follow our lead, people will learn that if they want a job, they have to clean up their lives").

Each of the 234 respondents that test was brought to its policy by a unique combination of conditions and concerns. The data allow one to generalize, however. If there are fork lifts, oil rigs, 18-wheelers, or high-speed machinery to be operated, bet that the company has talked about drug testing. If the company has this kind of equipment and is very large, the chances are 50-50 that it is testing some employees, at least at some sites.

Company size influences matters simply because larger firms have more resources (medical, legal, human resources, employee assistance, and the like) to assign to the likely first step—formulating a policy.

POLICY ISSUES

Most of our respondents see a written testing policy as the cornerstone for an effective testing program. They have edged toward testing cautiously, with a corporate task force to study the issues. They have a clear rationale for their actions, and a program to communicate the policy to company workers. Asked what they would recommend to others introducing testing programs, the large company respondents repeatedly emphasized issues of planning, policy, and communication. "It's a four-legged stool," said one midwestern manufacturer. "First, deterrence; second, medical screening; third, education and referrals; and fourth, treatment. All of these have to be aspects of a single policy, and all have to be communicated if the problem is going to be addressed."

Others agree. "Know what you're doing and why you're doing it. Have a good *business reason* for doing it." "Don't let policy develop bottom up, as happened here when one of our units started testing. Develop the policy at the top, then send it out as a complete package." "Study it—find out how the troops are going to act. We used a grapevine-buzzgroup approach, asking people in the plants to talk about it with employee groups, then monitor the responses." "Plan slowly, with a lot of involvement at every level, salaried and unsalaried, union and nonunion. The policy must precede testing. Testing is just a tool in an overall approach to dealing with abuse, an approach that must include education and treatment." And so on.

Most of this advice is based on recent experience. Nine out of ten respondent companies that test inaugurated those policies in 1985 or '86, as Exhibit 1.4 makes clear.

Much information has already reached print on the importance of a written policy, and workplace education manuals and audiovisual packages (see Chapter 3) are adding still more. Committee work does, indeed, pay off in documentation that the company has thought through the issues and acted in a responsible manner. Policy statements spell out the company's position on drug use and abuse, list consequences of drug use on the job, and provide a clear statement

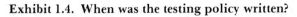

Exhibit 1.4. When was the testing policy written?

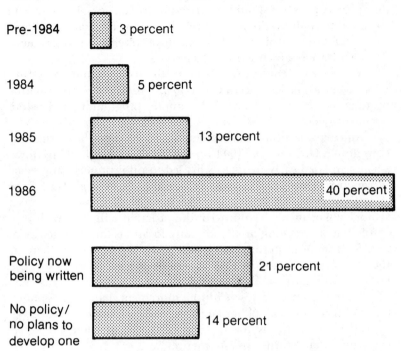

Pre-1984 — 3 percent

1984 — 5 percent

1985 — 13 percent

1986 — 40 percent

Policy now being written — 21 percent

No policy/ no plans to develop one — 14 percent

of provisions for rehabilitation. Such statements are themselves tools, according to the respondents.

Yet the policy-writing stage seems to stall many firms. Consider this, from a small food processing company on the West Coast:

> Being a fairly young company, we are still very much in the developing stages. Our policies are written by a policy committee, reviewed through legal counsel, and finally approved by our senior staff. Our committee is now attempting to tackle preemployment policy and would like to include drug testing. With all the legal issues today and no clear answers to all the questions, we are finding it very difficult to complete.

The respondent also explained that, to deal with matters until policy is formulated, the company president staged several mandatory meetings to state the firm's stand on alcohol and drugs, as well as provisions for help. "Employees were made well aware that if a disciplinary problem should get to the point of dismissal, it is too late to request rehabilitation." The rehabilitation program is offered through a local hospital, and the employee receives a full paycheck during a leave of absence (up to 30 days).

Many large firms, as well, told us that considering the testing issue had awakened a concern with rehabilitation. "We're overdue for setting up an EAP," said one. "We want the program in place before we start testing."

And many large manufacturers have found the policy formation slow going. One *Fortune* 100 firm told us that the initial task force was formulated early in 1986. This led to pilot projects in preemployment screening at six company locations. An expanded task force then formulated a five-step implementation recommendation for senior management. If approved, the program will start with preemployment screening at all company locations (all samples to be processed at one centralized laboratory). After a period of evaluation, the firm will centralize its EAP function, then move into for-cause testing, and finally, random testing.

The description of slow, cautious movement characterizes policy formation at almost all of our large company respondents. It applies as well to the majority (68 percent) of the smaller and mid-sized companies that returned questionnaires.

What about policy writing in the others, which make up almost one-third of our database? Many of these have opted to write their testing policies *concurrent* with program implementation. Policy will solidify after a pilot stage. Others (13 percent) say they have no policy—and no plans to develop one—yet they are testing. Given the storm clouds gathering in the legal arena, such practices seem risky. It's possible, of course, to have a clearly thought out rationale for testing even though there is no written policy. Sort through the numbers, give the no answers the benefit of doubt, and it turns out that approximately one out of ten firms now testing is doing so without benefit of written policy or clear rationale.

WHO IS CONSULTED ON POLICY DEVELOPMENT?

To answer this question, we gave the respondents a nine-item checklist of functional areas that might well have input into the decision making. (The list was drawn from recommendations made by various consultants on who should serve on such a task force.) Respondents could check as many categories as applicable and write in "other" functions. A follow-up question asked which of these functions played a leadership role in policy development. Exhibit 1.5 gives the results of both questions.

Exhibit 1.5. Task force membership and the leadership role.

Who was consulted during the process of policy development?

Function	Percentage checking "yes"
Senior management	84
Legal department or consultant	79
Human resources	90
In-house medical staff	31
Medical consultant, nonstaff	46
Health and safety officer	25
Security officers	18
Employee assistance program	27
Union representatives	19
All others	10

Notes: Respondents could check as many categories as needed. Because the group may have drawn more than one representative from each area, the percentages cannot be used to calculate total number on the task force. Respondents with "no policy-no plans to develop one" were excluded from the calculation.

Which of the above functions played the leadership role in policy development?

Function	Percentage checking this category
Senior management	21
Legal staff/consultant	4
Human resources	58
In-house medical	3
Health and safety	3
Security officer	1
EAP	1
No answer/responsibility divided	8

Human resources led the activity in 58 percent of the cases, senior management in 21 percent, and leadership was divided among several areas in 8 percent. In only 3 percent of the companies did the legal and medical consultants play the leadership role, and in only a handful of cases did the EAP take the lead.

Again, it seems that the majority of respondents followed recommended procedures in bringing together an interdisciplinary task force. Again, there are some alarming flares in the data. Twenty-one percent did not bring a lawyer into the planning stage; about the same number did not consult a medical adviser, either on-staff or from outside. Unlikely as it may seem, 10 percent did not bring the human resources staff into the planning process.

Our researchers shared preliminary findings on this question with professionals in both the medical and legal fields—producing predictable outrage. "There are so many complex issues, just in the type of test and the lab procedures, that it's absolutely unthinkable to go into this without consulting a medical person," said one of the doctors. "This is the best argument I've heard for putting a medical person on company staff," said another—himself a doctor.

One additional point: approximately 40 percent of our respondents indicated (in response to a latter question) that their companies had EAP programs, either in-house or in a consortium arrangement. Yet only 26 percent consulted the EAP in policy development. This means that in many cases (14 percent of the firms studied) the task force sidestepped the EAP.

A number of authors in the EAP field have scorned such practices, pointing out that of all functions in the corporate universe, no area is better qualified to deal with substance abuse issues. After all, its the EAP professional who has spent a lifetime handling substance abuse referrals—many with impressive success rates.

Of potentially greater concern to the EAP professional is the finding that many of the testing programs (60 percent) function without benefit of an active employee assistance program. There can, of course, be an "EAP like" function—someone in personnel, for example, might lend a sympathetic ear, then recommend treatment by a local hospital, consistent with company policy.

There is, however, a very clear correlation in the data between the absence of an EAP and automatic termination for substance abuse. Although respondents with such practices form a small portion of our database, virtually all are operating without EAP functions. Only two companies with EAPs tend toward automatic termination.

But isn't the EAP a corporate-giants-only phenomenon? Not so, if we consider the more recent developments in consortium and other shared-resource EAPs, a topic discussed in Chapter 4. About 10 percent of our respondents indicated that they have arranged for EAP services through such facilities.

GOT A POLICY? TELL THE WORLD

Once the policy is written, it should be communicated to the employees—standard "textbook advice" given in any number of magazine and journal articles treating the subject.

Again, the majority (60 percent) feel that they have done a thorough job of telling employees about the policy. On average, these respondents tell us that about 90 percent of their workers have received written statements.

What do we say about the others—the puzzling 40 percent that have not communicated policy in written form? A number of smaller firms noted that they had communicated policy orally, in stand-up meetings. Other companies simply have no policy worth communicating. Still others are in a trial stage, and policy will crystallize (and be communicated) once they find their bearings and firm up their programs. And still others have, apparently, opted not to communicate policy even though they have one.

Some guidelines for policy development have been written in the courtroom. Chapter 2 will look at several cases in which firms engaged in secret drug testing during employees' annual physical exams. But this, of course, applies to testing of current employees. Some of the respondents in the category of having a written—but hidden—policy are engaged in preemployment screening only. Does the communication principle apply in this case?

Yes, say many of our respondents: that's one of the objectives. Once the word gets out that companies are testing, fewer users will apply. Employers send a clear message to the community by making their preemployment testing programs public—and the greater the public awareness, the more effective the program. "We post large signs in the waiting room," said one respondent. "You can't get a job application without seeing a public notice that all candidates will be tested." And every drug user who doesn't apply is one fewer "positive" that needs to be validated.

Many in this camp are well aware that program effectiveness will diminish over time, as applicants develop the control to stay straight for a month before applying. But even that means that the program is having an impact, say the respondents.

WHAT HAPPENS TO THE CANDIDATE WHO TESTS POSITIVE?

No job offer. And if the candidate refuses to take the test (a legal right), he or she is not even considered. This is how the vast majority of firms handle matters. Some companies (about 10 percent) make provisions for a second test after a short waiting period. Some may hire with a specified period of probation, with the employee subjected to periodic testing. This practice, however, is not widespread—used by only about 2 percent of our respondents.

Our 234 respondents are experiencing a 15 percent "positive rate" in nonexempt candidates, about 9 percent for the exempts. However, several respondents told us of rejection rates of upwards of 50 percent.

How information on test results should be handled points toward another concern: should a candidate be told about a positive test?

Yes, according to the "consensus report" from the National Institute for Drug Abuse (NIDA). The objective in all cases should be education and rehabilitation, and for this reason applicants who test positive should be told about it, say the advisers who formulated the NIDA report. One *Fortune* 100 respondent told us that his policy will not be implemented until all persons who do the recruiting and interviewing are trained in how to talk to candidates about the test—and how to inform a candidate of a positive result.

No, say about 25 percent of the companies studied. These firms simply deny employment to candidates. No job. No reason given. Some may feel that public awareness will start a cat and mouse game—the test of "smarts and straights" referred to in the introduction. Although the employment-at-will doctrine may be eroding, there's still no rule on the books that says an employer must tell an applicant why employment was denied.

WHO IS BEING TESTED—AND FOR WHAT REASONS?

To investigate the "who and why" in testing, AMA researchers drew on a concept proposed by Dr. Dale Masi and Laura B. Burns in the EAP Digest (October, 1986). Masi and Burns suggest that each job can be examined in terms of its sensitivity—the impact drug-related impairment would have—in four distinct areas:

- Public safety—that is, the safety of the clients and customers served;
- Workplace safety—that is, the safety of fellow workers and employees;
- The ability to perform work;
- The public trust—that is, the confidence bestowed in certain types of jobs.

The latter rationale refers to the kind of confidence placed in doctors, government officials, pilots and air traffic controllers, school teachers, bankers, police officers, and others to whom well-being is entrusted.

Using these four categories as guides, an employer can begin to think through the possible impact of on-the-job impairment, assess impact, refine the rationale, and work out a testing approach that would make sense. For a bus driver, for example, the rationale clearly falls into the category of public safety, the cost impact of impairment would be significant, and a program of both preemployment screening and for-cause testing might be judged as appropriate.

Our questionnaire listed these four categories, plus one additional category: morale. We asked respondents to classify their rationales into these five slots for both preemployment and current-employee testing. The question also gave respondents opportunity to write in an "other." "Workplace security/theft prevention" was the most frequent write-in. Exhibit 1.6 shows the results, along with indication of which applicant groups are being tested.

Although "morale" is far less tangible than the other impact areas, a number of firms consulted during the study-planning stage told us that this was clearly a motivation.

Many employers do not discriminate by position in preemployment screening. All candidates get screened, regardless of what risk the job involves. There are currently no legal restrictions on this type

Exhibit 1.6. Preemployment testing practices.

Rationales cited for testing, in order of frequency

Workplace safety	72 Percent
Impairment/productivity	57
Public safety	42
Workplace morale	22
Public trust	13
National security	13

How preemployment screening is applied

All new hires, regardless of level or position	80 Percent
Hourly workers only	5
Selected job categories only	15

Note: N=211. Calculations exclude respondents doing current-employee testing only.

of testing, although curtailment may come at some future date (see the next chapter). There is, however, a growing body of legal argument supporting the right of both private and public sector employers to screen applicants for critical and sensitive jobs. The question of noncritical jobs is yet to be tested.

In this regard, the National American Wholesale Grocers Association (NAWGA) recommends the following to its 500 member companies: "As a general rule, NAWGA believes that preemployment screening is a desirable step which should be considered by member companies *for employees who drive trucks or operate dangerous equipment* [emphasis added]. Public safety, the safety of co-workers, and the security of company property and interests justify such actions."

Current employees may be tested on a random or periodic basis, or for cause. Exhibit 1.7 shows how such testing is applied, and lists the rationales—the categories, as above—for performing such tests. Still another query attempted to determine if employees who accepted promotions and/or transfers were subjected to testing. Those results also appear in Exhibit 1.7.

Employers are much more selective in the application of current-employee testing, with for-cause being the most frequent application.

Exhibit 1.7. Current-employee testing practices.

Rationales used, in order of frequency.

Workplace safety	53 Percent
Improvement/productivity	46
Public safety	31
Morale	15
Public trust	10
National security	4

How is random, periodic, and for-cause testing applied to current employees?

	Number of respondents		
	For cause	Periodic	Random
All employees	134	10	15
Selected levels (e.g., hourly workers).	35	7	3
Selected jobs (e.g., those involving safety)	43	17	7

Are employees who accept transfers subject to testing?

Yes, all employees	6 Percent
Yes, but only selected positions	10
No	84

Notes: All calculations apply to the 178 respondents who do current employee testing. For example, 134 respondents apply for-cause testing to all employees. Virtually all others do for-cause testing for selected levels or selected jobs. (Because a respondent might check both selected levels and selected jobs, the total exceeds 178). Of potential interest is the small—but significant—number that apply periodic and random testing to all employees.

This comes as no surprise. This practice, with a longer history than any of the prior methods, remains far less controversial. Some firms administer such tests after any kind of accident, others make it a distinct possibility.

The term "for cause" is frequently applied to situations in which a supervisor notes suspicious conduct—excessive lateness, marked deterioration of performance, and the like. A number of the people interviewed noted that, in their companies, the decision to test or not to test rested in the hands of the medical department. "A supervisor is not a policeman." A supervisor sees only impaired performance; it's up to the medical department to decide if a test is warranted—and it's up to the EAP to provide an avenue for rehabilitation. Confusion of these roles leads to trouble, according to the respondents.

There are more legal crosscurrents flowing here. An employer is obligated to exercise reasonable care in the selection, retention, and supervision of employees, and failure to do so can lead to negative exposure and liability. If an employer fails to exercise such reasonable care in the case of, say, a drug-impaired truck driver, an injured plaintiff can collect plenty. On the other hand, arbitrary and capricious testing may constitute invasion of privacy. This is not a matter of being "between a rock and a hard place"; the terrain is spongy on both sides. The presence of a drug testing program, in itself, would be feeble evidence that an employer has exercised reasonable and proper supervision.

Still, there is a dilemma in the conflicting arguments, and both point to litigation. This context makes the employer's rationale for testing paramount.

The areas of random and periodic testing are currently spotted with legal minefields, and companies considering this kind of testing are directed to Chapter 2 and, by all means, to their own corporate counsel.

SPEAKING OF PILOTS . . .

> "I'm dead set against the idea of mandatory drug testing -- right up
> to the time I get onto an airplane."

> - A civil liberties lawyer

While half of the nation's 100 largest industrial firms screen job applicants for drugs, far fewer perform random or periodic tests on current employees. Of the dozen that do (or plan to begin in 1987), all restrict the effort to specific job categories.

"What categories?" AMA researchers asked.

"Pilot," came the invariable answer. Each listed a variety of other jobs—security personnel, drivers, machinists—but all of them listed "pilot"—and all of them listed it first.

Beyond our polling efforts, AMA staffers discussed mandatory drug testing with hundreds of others: occupational health and safety experts, employee relations specialists, personnel and human relations officers. Many could see good arguments both for and against periodic tests—and most of the arguments for regular testing began, "Well, airline pilots, for example . . ."

But the Federal Aviation Administration does not mandate testing for airline pilots, and has just begun to test air traffic controllers.

And the airline industry, having submitted its own proposal to the FAA about testing pilots, flight crews, and other personnel, is waiting for word—waiting for a far longer time than they had anticipated.

The FAA Tests Its Own

In 1985, the FAA took up the issue of periodic drug testing and formed a task force to answer two separate but related questions: should the FAA test any or all of its own employees? And, further, should it mandate tests for pilots and others who work in the airline industry, which operates under FAA regulation?

The FAA task force was a large one: nearly two dozen people were assigned, including the federal air surgeon, the chief counsel, and the associate administrator for air traffic, whose divison represents about half of the FAA workforce. Their key concerns: to ensure safety in air travel and transport and to see that the FAA's 45,000 employees suffered no job impairment due to drug use.

In late 1985, the task force issued its recommendations, which were endorsed by the administrator. Drug or alcohol use on the job became grounds for automatic dismissal. Drug or alcohol abuse off the job that resulted in impairment earned employees a directive to enter an FAA rehabilitation program; refusal to enter the program was grounds for dismissal.

Testing entered the picture a year later. The FAA already required an annual physical examination for many of its employees; as of January 1, 1987, a drug test became part of that exam. The new rule applied to workers whose jobs were directly related to flight safety: air traffic controllers, aircraft inspectors, federal air marshals and security personnel, and pilots of the FAA's own aircraft. Together, these people represent 15 percent of the FAA's complement. At the same time, tests were required upon "reasonable suspicion" of drug abuse.

But none of these new rules applied to workers employed by the airline industry itself—neither those who flew the airplanes nor those who maintained them. To the task force, it was the FAA's job to ensure that FAA regulations were observed: that aircraft are airworthy, and that pilots are fit for duty. The manner in which that is done, however, was up to the individual airlines—"best left to the discretion of the industry."

And the industry was at work in the same vineyard.

The Industry Takes Up the Issue

The Air Transport Association of America, headquartered in Washington D.C., represents all major domestic carriers. It is through the ATA that the airline industry speaks to the public and deals with regulatory agencies of government—the FAA foremost among them. Within the ATA, industrywide standards are set and applications made to the FAA for changes in regulations.

In 1986, a panel of chief executive officers of the airline industry met with Vice President George Bush to discuss ways and means to a drug-free work environment. At the time, most airlines included drug screening in preemployment physical examinations; a positive finding usually meant withdrawal of the job offer. But most airlines had no policy with respect to current employees—no random or periodic testing, and no testing for cause.

Urged by the Vice President, the airlines created a multidisciplinary task force, coordinated by the ATA's general counsel, James Landry. Along with the familiar issues of cost, test accuracy, and privacy rights, the committee had to deal with a central question: would the industry police itself in drug-related matters, or would it request a new regulation from the FAA, which would then be responsible for its enforcement?

The task force straddled the fence. Though most of its members leaned toward a petition for a new regulation, that avenue seemed to run counter to the deregulatory philosophy of the administration and the trend in the industry itself. Therefore, the ATA task force put together a "policy statement" and forwarded the draft to the ATA board of directors.

But the directors tossed the ball back to the task force. This was indeed a matter for FAA regulation, said the directors, because it was important to have the policy backed with the force of law. This followed the lead of the Federal Railroad Administration (FRA), which had promulgated rules on substance abuse in 1985, and watched those rules withstand a district court challenge.

The FRA rules, copied by the ATA task force:

- Prohibit employees from using drugs or alcohol on the job, or from reporting for work under their influence.
- Enforce testing for all safety-related jobs—which in the airline industry would encompass almost all airport personnel save ticket clerks and baggage handlers—on reasonable suspicion of job impairment.
- Mandate drug testing after any accident or safety-related incident.
- Grant at least one opportunity for rehabilitation to employees who voluntarily seek assistance for substance abuse.

The ATA proposal featured two additional points. There would be minimum requirements industrywide, with each particular carrier entitled to enter into periodic or random testing of air crews and ground personnel. Moreover, the FAA rules would be nationally applicable, and preempt state or local ordinances that might prohibit testing. A recently passed ordinance in San Francisco was very much in mind in the latter recommendation.

Finally, the task force's work had board approval. At this point, the ATA submitted the proposals to unions representing airline pilots, machinists, and flight attendants; all found the concept generally acceptable.

Then, in June 1986, the ATA met with the FAA and its parent, the Department of Transportation. But by that time, the ATA's drive to petition the FAA for a formal rule had been blunted. Instead, the proposals were submitted informally, as "food for thought," according to an ATA spokesman.

And from that time through the end of 1986, the Department of Transportation has considered the proposal. The latest word, says the ATA, is that the department intends to put out its own notice of rule-making, which "may or may not" follow the guidelines provided by the ATA's task force.

The changes and delays are an irritant to one participant in the

33

process. "The issue isn't job impairment," said the source. "It would be simpler if it were limited to job impairment. But drug use is illegal, period. This is a societal problem that has to be dealt with. The issue is drug use *per se*."

WALKING AROUND THE MODESTY ISSUE

In many cases of random testing, samples are collected on company premises—driving dead center into one of the most difficult of side issues.

Methods of collecting samples can bump hard against commonly accepted standards of decency. The problem: to assure sample integrity, someone must watch the employee (or candidate) void into the sample bottle.

Perhaps if a test other than the immunoassay method were in vogue, the issues would be less thorny. No one feels humiliated if asked to part with a small lock of hair or give a few drops of blood. But it's the immunoassay method that's now the marketplace method of favor, and that means collecting a urine sample.

Is observation really necessary? Yes, assuming that the employer wants to make sure that he is getting a true test. Are persons actually capable of a deceptive sample switch? Absolutely. Drug abusers are capable of making a switch, especially so if a job is at stake.

Columnist Jimmy Breslin, writing in the *New York Daily News*, made many people aware of this practice by telling the story of a young man, a financial analyst, who had just received the promotion of a lifetime. He was ecstactic—until he learned that he had to take a drug test. As the story (apparently true) goes, he successfully made the switch—holding a vial of "clean" urine under hot tapwater before handing it to the doctor.

Rumor has it that a "guaranteed clean" sample has a street value of about $80 in New York and that a California company is now marketing easily concealable carrying devices. These devices allow a person to carry the clean sample discreetly hidden, even when disrobed. (See also, box, p. 35.)

Despite the opportunity to cheat where samples are being collected on company premises (the case for about one out of four companies), the majority of companies *do not make it a practice to have someone watch the person void*. Twenty-nine percent do.

We put the question of observation to a number of our *Fortune* 100 respondents. Several, quite frankly, answered with the idea that "sometimes you just have to trust people. If you start suspecting everything, then there's no end to the amount of deception you can impute to human conduct." Others reported that observation has become an accepted practice.

"Nickle Bags, Nickle Bags. . ."

Next time you hear this whisper on the street, don't assume it's your neighborhood drug dealer. There's an active black market in clean urine specimens.

In Texas, it's all above board. Byrd Laboratories of Austin provides "guaranteed 100 percent substance-free urine" by mail order at $49.95 per.

Advertised in the *Austin Chronicle*, the Byrd product promises "no additives, no drug impurities, no foreign agents of any kind." At a future date, the stuff will be delivered "freeze-dried; just add water." It's hyped as "suitable for unanticipated urine demand."

Wasn't "Be Prepared" once the Boy Scout motto?

Sands of Iwo Jima?

Word from a serving U.S. Marine: "Four grains of salt dropped into urine sample will nullify the specimen." The favored hiding place in the Corps, which initiated periodic testing in 1985: under the fingernails.

Several, however, pointed to a more creative solution—controlling the circumstances. The employee or candidate, clad in an examination gown, steps into a "dry room," to give the sample, then hands it to the attendant before stepping into the bathroom to wash hands. In situations where such control is warranted, this practice—or something like it—may provide the route around a sensitive problem. And those "discreet hiding devices" referred to earlier? If the sample is taken during a physical exam, the doctor conducts all other steps in the examination prior to asking for the sample.

This doesn't apply to situations in which samples are requested in the plant or at some other company location—an oil refinery, for example. Yes, an unannounced test may take an employee by surprise, thus avoiding a sample switch. But that's leaving much to chance. Thus, observation is necessary, say many consultants. If it is not handled with respect for the employee, it can cause problems. One respondent who is facing a lawsuit on this issue (the employees, working in a high-risk situation, were fired for refusing to give a sample in front of a witness) feels that the company's case will be strengthened significantly by a number of factors: a clearly written rationale spelling out the risks involved in the job, a well publicized program of help for persons with drug problems, and evidence from other sources that the employees were using drugs in the plant.

TEST ACCURACY—BOGUS ISSUE, OR CAUSE FOR CONCERN?

"Many people fear that drug screening may result in accusation of innocent people," states Peter B. Chapin of the Human Relations Institute and Clinics in Washington, D.C. "This fear is justified," according to Chapin.

But each of AMA's *Fortune* 100 respondents who test told us that they perform one of several alternative tests (thin layer chromatography, gas chromatography, or gas chromatography/mass spectrometry) on all positives. Ninety percent of our questionnaire respondents who test do the same.

No other aspect of the problem has received wider publicity. And the termination of employment on the basis of an unconfirmed test is an almost sure guarantee that a subpoena will arrive soon. For the moment, let's say only that much of the bad press surrounding immunoassay tests grew out of statistically valid studies conducted by the U.S. Navy, the Centers for Disease Control, Northwestern University, and others. In each case the organization tested the testers by controlling the samples sent to various laboratories for testing. The error rate—in terms of false positives—averaged from the 25 percent up to 60 percent.

The problem is not solely with the test itself. The manufacturers claim a 95 to 97 percent accuracy rate—under the best lab conditions. First, however, the employer and laboratory need to agree on a threshold, measured in billionths of a gram per mililiter, for the amount of any substance that will be ruled as a "positive." Problems enter because of human errors (poorly trained or careless technicians), equipment problems, and improper shipping and handling. Some labs have, reportedly, set the calibrations low—enough to catch only chronic users—in order to avoid an overly high rejection rate and potential accusations from employers about poor technique and false positives.

Taking the manufacturers at their word, a 97 percent accuracy rate means that three out of every hundred new hires will test falsely in preemployment screening. The false positives can be retested by more sophisticated (and more expensive) methods. *The false negatives are generally not validated.*

Rapid increases in the number of laboratories processing the immunoassay test, spurred by news of a high-growth market, exacerbate the sore spot. Many of these firms may be ill-equipped and poorly staffed, offering a corporate client less than satisfactory accuracy and turnaround time. Or so the critics charge.

Asked what advice they would give to other firms installing such tests, respondents ranked "selection of a competent lab" second only to "careful planning and policy formulation." Several noted that they had changed laboratories. The false-positive rate was leading to unwarranted expenses for confirmatory tests. In addition, administrative hassles, turnaround time, and bureaucratic problems had created undue frustration. "There's just no way of imposing quality control on the lab," said one respondent. "You have to trust people. But that doesn't always work. The lab can see you coming—and start covering up. That's what happened to us."

Claims to the contrary notwithstanding, test accuracy is a concern, and the fears expressed by the American Civil Liberties Union and others are wellfounded and quite valid. *Approximately 8 percent of our respondents told us that they are not confirming initial tests with any kind of more sophisticated technology.* True, this is a small number compared to the total number of companies testing. Still, while the problem might not be as widespread as some critics assert, it does exist.

The accuracy issue walks hand in hand with the issue of cost,

Exhibit 1.8. Drugs targeted for testing.

Cocaine	85 Percent
Heroin	79
Marijuana	85
Valium	67
Other	36

given the expense of validation. "The red flags went up as soon as we started putting money in the budget," said one respondent. This may not, however, be indicative of a trend. Only about 2 percent of the firms now testing foresee program curtailment within the next five years.

Our questionnaire also asked respondents to indicate what drugs they routinely targeted in testing. Exhibit 1.8 gives the results.

And if the result is positive, who is told? Privacy laws differ from state to state. Some hold that all such information is protected by the privileged doctor-patient relationship; others allow wider distribution of job-related test results. Exhibit 1.9 gives the results without reference to regional differences in the law.

WHAT HAPPENS TO AN EMPLOYEE WITH A SUBSTANCE ABUSE PROBLEM?

By the slightest of margins—10 percent to 7.7 percent—companies that test are more likely to issue a ticket out of the workplace. But by the same token, companies that test are slightly more inclined to offer rehabilitation; again the margin is close—68 percent to 65 percent.

Exhibit 1.9. If an employee tests positive, who is informed of the results? (Percentage saying yes, this person is informed).

The employee	79 Percent
The EAP	31
Medical department	29
Personnel	71
Security	05
The employee's manager	61

Attempts to get a finer reading on this were frustrated by the great variety of practices. The action taken is often conditioned by circumstances: the type of work involved, the employee's past work record, whether this is a first offense, and the like. Thus, many of the respondents bypassed the check-list and wrote in answers, making computer analysis difficult. The drug abuser may be asked to leave the workplace for a specified period of time, returning only with a medical certification that the problem is under control. One respondent put it this way: "If the employee admits he has a problem, we offer rehabilitation. If we find it out, he's fired." The firm's self-referral rate has jumped by some 50 percent since policy implementation. Some respondents noted that an employee who shows signs of drug abuse is tested periodically for a specified period after he or she is referred to the EAP.

"It depends on the person," wrote one candid respondent. "If he's an hourly worker, we usually fire. If he's a manager, we'd probably give him help." Still another reason for a carefully formulated policy.

How are referrals handled? Exhibit 1.10 gives answers to this question. If the firm does not have an EAP, referrals are handled by the medical department or personnel.

Many of our respondents emphasized the importance and utility of working through an EAP, and several told us that they had started EAP programs concurrent with their testing programs. For most of our large-company respondents, an effective EAP is an essential "context" for testing. It's a ready resource for other program components—training of supervisors, for example, and a cost-effective center for helping troubled employees regain their standing. Those companies that do not have EAPs are handling the referrals through the personnel function.

Exhibit 1.10. Which function handles drug-related referrals?

EAP (in house)	31 Percent
Consortium/network EAP	10
Physician/medical department	12
Personnel	25
Other	4
No answer	19

When all else fails, termination is inevitable. The employee may refuse treatment, or regress back to old habits after a period of rehabilitation. We put one additional, very simple question to our respondents: Have you ever fired an employee for drug abuse? Yes, say 49 percent of the respondents. Compare this with companies that are not currently testing, where only about 26 percent say they have fired for drug abuse. Quite clearly, companies that engage in testing are more likely to terminate employees on the basis of drug abuse.

Of course, far more than a test result has to be involved. There has to be "just cause" for a supervisor to refer the employee in the first place. As one respondent put it, in telling how he measured effectiveness, "Testing gives you a very important lever for tipping the situation one way or another—the employee either goes to counseling . . . or out the door."

This is one of several ways to measure effectiveness—a subject treated below. If the foregoing discussion has seemed to emphasize the negative aspects of testing, it was only to bring out the myriad problems that need to be dealt with. After listening to the respondents and looking at the evidence, we have to conclude that drug testing can be a useful tool.

TODAY AND TOMORROW

More than half the companies that currently engage in testing expect to continue their current policies for the foreseeable future; a tiny 3 percent envision a gradual phase out. An important segment of the sample (see Exhibit 1.11) looks toward a mandate for expansion. Companies that currently test for cause expect to begin preemployment screening; those that check applicants see a move into random or periodic testing.

Exhibit 1.11. In your judgment, what will happen to your testing program within the next five years?

Stay the same	56 Percent
Expand, to cover other groups	24
Phase out/diminish	3
Uncertain/no answer	16

But only a bare majority of respondents who test feel that the effort is an effective tool in dealing with workplace substance abuse (see Exhibit 1.12). Some find their current practices insufficient; as above, they would like to expand the range of their programs. Others emphasize, once again, that testing is but one facet of a wider effort against drugs. Testing for cause, these respondents say, merely identifies the problem; rehabilitative services treat it. Respondents with education and awareness programs are more positive about testing—confirming the "four-legged stool" metaphor cited earlier. Naturally, companies that have just begun to test are less convinced of its effectiveness than those with long experience.

It is no easy task to measure the effectiveness of any drug prevention program. The questionnaire asked respondents what sort of objective measurements might be used, over time, to gauge program impact. We put the same question to a number of our *Fortune* 100 respondents. Only four respondents told us that data collection was under way. Such matters as accident rates, insurance claims, absenteeism, worker's compensation claims, referrals to an EAP, and the like, tracked over a period of time, would provide the answers.

Several dozen of our small-company respondents noted that they had already achieved reductions in at least one of these areas. Many, however, listed more subjective approaches. This response, from a California company, summarizes many of the opinions:

Exhibit 1.12. In your judgment, is the program effective in helping to solve a real problem?

Total sample:

Yes	55 Percent
No	30
Uncertain	15

Sample segment: If respondent has educational program in place.

Yes	60 Percent
No	27
Uncertain	12

N=234

1. Our industrial accidents have decreased dramatically.
2. Quality of work has improved.
3. Preemployment applicants "are less dirty" as time goes by (i.e., fewer applicants test positive).
4. Several of our employees have come forward and asked for help—in fact, have welcomed help.

Preemployment screening can cut both ways. Some respondents believe that a stable or rising rate of positives among candidates would justify the program, in that each drug user not hired is one less potential problem. A diametrically opposite view would see a drop in the number of positives as proof that the program was doing its job as a deterrent. Heads, the idea is effective; tails, it's effective.

A surprising number of respondents, representing companies of all sizes, indicated that preemployment screening was intended as a statement of the firm's commitment to a drug-free workplace. The objective, then, relates to company image and a concept of corporate citizenship, making measurement difficult.

KEEPING COUNT

How many employees have been referred to an EAP or other resource for drug-related rehabilitation within the past year? our questionnaire asked. *What increase or decrease does this represent over the prior year?*

A clear policy, an offer of rehabilitation, and the presence of a testing program can increase the rate of referrals. And this increase is more likely to happen if the company is engaged in some kind of drug testing—or so respondents *report*. Many of the respondents, however, were not able to report rate-increase data, and thus the results may prove only that companies now testing are more likely to have data available. (In many cases, this information is confidential, or the statistics may include drug and alcohol abuse in the same category.) See Exhibit 1.13 for what data is available.

Comparisons based simply on the number of referrals, however, shore up credibility. Companies with drug abuse programs in which testing is one component produce significantly more referrals than the non-testing firms. About half of the respondents were able to supply data for this question, and the distribution along lines of

Exhibit 1.13. Respondents reporting increases in rate of drug-related referrals within the past year.

	Companies testing (Percent)	Companies not testing (Percent)
Increase in referral rate	19	13
Decrease in referral rate	5	2
No answer	77	85

N=234

company size makes a comparison possible. See Exhibit 1.14.

The most significant relationship in the data, however, is not the correlation between testing and the number of referrals. Rather, the dramatic leap comes in the relationship with an educational and training program. Among companies now testing, the referral rate triples if the supervisors have been trained in how to cope with work impairment.

In the process of reading through the open-ended responses and other comments written on the questionnaire, our researchers also noted a clear correlation between a strong policy and an increase in referrals.

Exhibit 1.14. Average number of referrals, past year.

	Companies testing	Companies not testing
Worksite population		
Fewer than 500	5	2
500 to 2,499	13	5
2,500 to 4,900	30	10
5,000 or more	52	28

Notes: 121 companies now testing (51 percent of the respondent base) provided answers
to this question; 406 companies *not* testing (48 percent) provided answers.

A Case in Point

> "I presented the drug testing idea in person. We knew that one person in the group had a problem, and suspected that another did as well. I said that we were going to start a testing program, and if anyone had a problem, they could save us all a lot of trouble by admitting it. We would provide help—and keep it confidential. Within a week, five people let me know they had problems."
>
> — CEO, respondent company

This story may not be typical. Nor is it intended as a model approach. But it makes a point. The employer did, indeed, have a problem. His policy was clear—and communicated in an effective way. The testing concept was explained in the context of help and rehabilitation. It worked.

By no means should this be taken as a blanket endorsement of drug testing. Based on what the respondents have told is, it is possible to rate preemployment screening as an effective tool for problem prevention, especially in positions where safety is a factor. And it is possible to see testing for cause as a valuable tool for helping to define a performance problem. In the latter case, much depends on how the phrase "for cause" (or "just cause," as it is sometimes called) is defined and approached. Both ideas point back to policy formation—and the careful analysis that must be undergone before program implementation.

Every company is different, every community is different—and so is every person. Any approach to workplace drug abuse must be flexible, and it must be adapted to the real need.

2

Workplace Drug Testing - The Legal Issues

Loren Siegel

WRITING ABOUT the legalities of drug testing in the workplace is a bit like playing a guessing game. Although the practice of urinalysis testing in American industry has, over the past year, experienced phenomenal growth, legal challenges in the private sector have only just begun. The situation is bound to change. As greater numbers of American workers are subjected to drug testing, many will feel they have been wronged—and will opt for litigation. But for now, any analysis of the legalities of testing in the private workplace must of necessity be based on analogy with the public sector, the identification of trends, and a healthy dose of informed speculation.

This chapter is divided into three major sections. The first deals with the urine tests themselves: Current drug testing technologies have certain inherent deficiencies, which in turn have legal ramifications. (For a detailed discussion of how the tests work and what they are and are not capable of revealing, see Appendix II.) The second section examines the legalities of drug testing in the public workplace. Unlike the private sector, public employment has been the arena for numerous legal challenges. A consensus is rapidly developing in the courts as to what may and may not be done within the constraints imposed by the United States Constitution. While these

About the Author

Attorney Loren Siegel is special assistant to the executive director, American Civil Liberties Union (ACLU). For the last year, she has been following the drug testing issue and has acted as the principle spokesperson for that organization.

decisions are not directly applicable to the private workplace, they do demonstrate how judges view a whole range of issues raised by the drug testing phenomenon and may presage future legislative action to regulate testing in private employment. The third and final section looks at a myriad of legal issues raised by private workplace drug testing, most of which have not yet been tested in the courts.

I. DRUG TESTING TECHNOLOGY

Although virtually all AMA survey respondents report that they are confirming all positive immunoassy tests, the limitations of this technology will continue to attract legal attention. Thus, some background is in order.

 Urine testing is, without question, the method of choice for the vast majority of companies, agencies and institutions (e.g., prisons and the military) conducting drug testing today. It is simpler and less expensive than blood tests, and, unlike brain scans and saliva analysis, urine testing is considered sound by a cross-section of the scientific/medical community.

The urine tests on the market today fall into two basic types: screening and confirmatory. Drug screens are highly sensitive and relatively inexpensive; confirmatory tests cost more and identify substances in the urine with greater specificity. There is unanimity among the experts, including the manufacturers of drug screening tests, that any positive result from a drug screen be subjected to confirmatory testing.

All enzyme immunoassays measure the amount of light given off in chemical reactions between an enzyme, an antibody, and the drug being tested for. Syva Corporation, for example, manufactures separate "kits" for 11 different drugs at a cost of between $6 and $11 each.

In addition to the low cost of the test itself, EMIT is particularly attractive to private industry because, according to its marketing literature, it does not require laboratory handling.

> "...because EMIT tests do not require specially licensed personnel, subjective interpretation of results or special handling techniques and safety precautions, they can be run by any trained staff member."

The second most common drug screen is the RIA (Radio Immunoassay) Abuscreen produced by Hoffman-LaRoche of Nutley, New Jersey. Most of Abuscreen's sales are to the military, which conducts more than one million tests per year. Like EMIT, RIA relies upon immunochemical processes, but since radioactive materials are used to identify substances in the urine, the services of licenced laboratories are required.

Drug screening is very much a growth industry, and numerous other pharmaceutical companies are jumping into the market with new products. Presumably, these products will have to rely upon the same technologies as EMIT and RIA and will therefore have the same fundamental strengths and weaknesses.

The standard, state-of-the-art *confirmatory* test goes by the acronym GC/MS, which stands for the unwieldy term, gas chromatography/mass spectometry. Unlike the immunoassays, GC/MS measures drug molecules directly by breaking the urine down into individual ions. Confirmatory tests must be conducted in a laboratory setting with special machinery and trained technicians. They are far more costly than the screening tests and can run from $60 to $100 per sample. The military runs confirmatory tests on all positive screen results. But because of the expense involved, private companies may be tempted not to follow up on positive screens, especially in the area of preemployment testing.

Are Screening Test Results Reliable?

In his article entitled, "Problems of Mass Urine Screening for Misused Drugs," John P. Morgan, M.D., described a major snafu in the Navy's drug testing program:

In 1982, the Navy began a massive urinary surveillance program. Naval laboratories increased their activities from 800 tests per month to 10,000 tests per month in each of four laboratories. By July 1982, a number of naval commanders began questioning the frequent occurrence of positive specimens. Six thousand positive urines reported between January and September 1982 were re-examined. Of these 6,000 samples, some 2,000 could not, according to the Navy publication *All Hands*, 'be scientifically substantiated as positive.' Another 2,000 samples were missing some form of documentation. This author has not learned whether these failures were in terms of chain of custody, handling of data, operator error, failure to confirm false positives or some combination thereof.

Although the Navy, a highly centralized and disciplined organization, was able to cure many of the defects in its drug testing program, others are simply consequences of an imperfect technology and cannot be remedied 100 percent. Experts worry about the enormous increase in workplace drug testing on an extremely decentralized basis, and the mounting pressures on laboratories to be competitive while handling an ever-expanding volume of samples. The reliability of the screening tests may well diminish substantially: "In a climate where there's money to be made, inevitably there will be incompetent and inadequately staffed laboratories," said Dr. Byron S. Finkle, a leading toxicologist at the University of Utah in Salt Lake City, during an interview with the *New York Times*. "The tests are very easy to do badly and very difficult to do well," he added.

Syva Corp., Abbott Laboratories, Hoffman-LaRoche, and other manufacturers claim a high rate of accuracy. Syva's literature, for example, states that the EMIT test can be used with a 95 to 97 percent confidence rate. This may be true under ideal laboratory conditions, but in the real world EMIT, RIA, and other screening tests may not perform that well. In 1983, inmates in New Jersey prisons sued the State Department of Corrections over the use of single, unconfirmed EMIT tests as a basis for disciplinary action. In preparation for the case, the department sent 400 positive EMIT tests for marijuana to a laboratory for confirmation by GC/MS. The EMIT tests had been run by a trained laboratory technician. Of the 400 positive EMIT tests, 107 were found to be false, yielding a false-positive rate of more than 25 percent. Other field tests have also indicated a higher rate of fallibility for both EMIT and RIA than their manufacturers concede. For example, Northwestern University in Chicago recently completed a study of positive EMIT tests for cocaine and found that 25 percent of the samples could not be confirmed.

False Positives

False positives—meaning the occurrence of positive test results when, in fact, the drug in question is not actually present in the urine—may be caused by several different factors. A major factor is the nonspecificity of the immunoassay technique, which picks up not only illegal substances, but similar chemical compounds as well. This phenomenon is called *cross-reactivity* and is very well documented in the case of the EMIT test. In February 1986 Syva Corporation informed its customers that three nonsteroidal, anti-inflammatory drugs, ibuprofen, fenoprofen, and naproxen, produced positive results on the EMIT marijuana test. The popular over-the-counter drugs Advil and Nuprin, among others, contain ibuprofen. Cold medications such as Contac and Sudafed may show up as amphetamines; Thorazine may show up as heroin and the antibiotic Amoxicillan as cocaine. Neither EMIT or RIA can distinguish between heroin and the legal drug codeine.

Certain foods and beverages can also produce false positives. In late 1985 the New Jersey state laboratory, investigating the complaints of several soldiers stationed at Fort Dix who had tested positive for marijuana, discovered that an oriental tea purchased and consumed by each of the men contained THC, the psychoactive ingredient in marijuana. The ingestion of poppy seed cake has produced a positive reading for opium. And there is evidence that if you have spent time in a room filled with marijuana smoke, even if you yourself have not smoked it, you may test positive for marijuana because of "passive inhalation."

False positives can even be caused by the fact that some people naturally excrete unusually large amounts of two enzymes (endogenous lysozyme and malate dehydrogenase) that are utilized in the EMIT test.

Because of the problem of false positives, several courts have held that the results of an unconfirmed EMIT test cannot be used as the sole basis for disciplinary action in the prison context. In another case, a federal court held that the termination of a school bus aide on the basis of one unconfirmed EMIT test was "arbitrary and capricious."

Confirmation of Test Results

Even the manufacturers of the screening test agree that positive test results ought to be confirmed by an alternate method (running the sample through a second immunoassay simply reproduces the erroneous result). The most frequently recommended confirmatory test, the GC/MS, which is currently used by the armed forces, is recommended by the Federal Alcohol, Drug Abuse and Mental Health Administration. While the test is highly accurate, it is also very expensive, running about $100 per sample. There are very few laboratories with highly specialized equipment required to conduct GC/MS. In 1983 the Navy spent $2 million to confirm 100,000 tests.

The expense of the confirmatory testing has steered some companies away from testing for drugs. James S. Kempner, Jr., former chairman of the Kempner Group, who recently participated in a panel on drug education at the 52nd annual Southern Governors Conference in Charlotte, N.C., stated his firm does not conduct drug testing anymore because of "the seeming unreliability; about 20 percent had to be retested." (*Washington Post*, 8/13/86).

Chain of Custody and Laboratory Quality Control

The accuracy of a drug testing program also depends on the extent to which a clear chain of custody can be established for every sample taken. Without a well-documented chain of custody, which protects against the switching, adulterating or mislabeling of samples, test results can easily be assailed as incorrect. This means that even the collection of the original urine sample must be closely observed by a witness. As Dr. Robert Newman, president of New York's Beth Israel Hospital, cautions, "A trusted worker must watch each person urinate into a bottle. If that is not done, it's a sham." (*New York Times*, 9/16/86). The samples must then be carefully labeled before they are transported to a laboratory.

Although the Syva Corporation claims that the EMIT assay can be analyzed at the worksite, experts counsel against entrusting this task to "undertrained personnel." Given the fact that even the best toxicology laboratories make errors with drug screens, both in terms of false positives and false negatives, it is probably unwise to think that nontechnical personnel can perform as well or better.

The studies of laboratory quality control in the area of mass drug testing programs have shown great disparities in the rates of accuracy. The most celebrated and oft-cited study was conducted by the Federal Centers for Disease Control between the years 1972 to 1981 and published in 1985 in the *Journal of the American Medical Association* under the title, "Crisis in Drug Testing." During the period of the study, scientists spiked urine samples collected at 262 methadone treatment centers around the country with various drugs. The samples were sent to 13 different clinical laboratories, some of which knew they were being tested, and some of which did not. The results were quite disappointing. The study, which used 80 percent accuracy in detecting evidence of drugs as an acceptable performance level, found that only one of 11 labs met the standard for barbiturates, zero of 12 for amphetamines, 6 of 12 for methadone, one of 11 for cocaine, 2 of 13 for codeine and one of 13 for morphine. There were substantially more false negatives than false positives. The study also found that the labs that knew they were being tested took greater care with the samples than those that did not know, suggesting that the regulation of laboratories is an important factor in insuring an acceptable level of quality control.

Today, however, mass screening programs for private industry are mainly being conducted not by clinical laboratories under some form of regulation, but by commercial labs which are, by and large, unregulated. On September 16, 1986, Dr. Lawrence Miike of Congress's Office of Technology Assessment testified before the House Post Office and Civil Service Committee on the subject of the "Accuracy and Reliability of Urine Drug Tests." Dr. Miike pointed out that:

> The extent and quality of laboratory regulation varies tremendously from state to state, and additionally, drug testing is not subject to as much regulation as clinical testing. It is quite easy to establish a drug testing laboratory with little or no monitoring by the state. The extent of regulation may also depend on the type of drug testing. For example, the RIA test, because it involves radioactive ingredients, is more regulated than is the EMIT test. Proficiency testing of labs that perform drug testing has found severe deficiencies in the past 10 years. . .Only a handful of states [New York, California, Pennsylvania and New Jersey] have proficiency testing programs.

In an effort to remedy this problem, the National Institute of Drug Abuse is planning to evaluate drug testing concerns and publish a list of laboratories that are up to standard. In the meantime, any company contemplating drug testing must be very wary of choosing a competent laboratory. Dr. Finkle of the University of Utah advises that there are only "about a dozen competent urine drug testing laboratories in the country." (*New York Times, 9/16/86*).

Can Urine Tests Show Job Impairment?

The simple answer to this query is, no. None of the urine tests can show job impairment or level of intoxication. They cannot show recency of use or how much of a drug was ingested. According to Richard L. Hawks of NIDA, "You cannot equate urine drug levels and impairment of performance. You can have a 20-fold variation in urine samples taken a few hours apart from the same individuals."

The inability of urine test to detect recency of use is a particular problem in the case of marijuana, the most commonly used illegal drug. Because of the way it is metabolized by the body, signs of marijuana can be detected more than a month after a regular user has stopped using it. The cocaine metabolite is eliminated from the body more rapidly, usually within four days after use. On the other hand, the tests cannot detect drugs that have just been ingested, because it takes several hours before the substance or its metabolites are eliminated in urine. Therefore it is possible that someone who quit smoking marijuana a month ago could test positive, whereas someone who snorted cocaine on the way to work could test negative.

The absence of a clear relationship between drug testing and job impairment is particularly galling to those who oppose testing on civil liberties grounds. "An employee who smokes a marijuana joint at a party on Saturday night may test positive the following Wednesday. So what?" writes the executive director of the American Civil Liberties Union, Ira Glasser. "Why is that his employer's business? And how does it differ from the employee who has a drink on Saturday night? What has that to do with his fitness to work five days later?" The ACLU views urinalysis as the unfair monitoring of employees' recreational activities off the job. Several labor arbitrators who have considered this issue have also been troubled by this problem. And in an opinion filed on September 18, 1986, Federal

Judge H. Lee Sarokin, in invalidating the testing of a group of public employees by the City of Plainfield, New Jersey, observed:

> We would be appalled at the spectre of the police spying on employees during their free time and then reporting their activities to their employers. Drug testing is a form of surveillance, albeit a technological one. Nonetheless, it reports on a person's off-duty activities just as surely as if someone had been present and watching. It is George Orwell's Big Brother Society come to life.

Given the range of problems associated with mass screening for drugs, and given present-day technology (including the rather significant problem of false *negatives*), companies must consider whether such screening is really efficacious. Generally it may not make sense to test large, unselected populations for rare events. In an article that appeared in *The Wall Street Journal* (4/14/86), Dr. William H. Anderson of Harvard University points out that a test with an accuracy rate of 95 percent will produce one wrong result for every 20 persons tested.

Recall that the vast majority of our survey respondents have, as part of their employee testing policies, reserved urinalysis for those workers who actually show job impairment. At the same time, the courts seem to be moving—however slowly—in the direction of allowable testing only when such a relationship is established.

II. DRUG TESTING IN PUBLIC EMPLOYMENT

On September 15, 1986, President Reagan issued his much anticipated executive order, "Drug-Free Federal Workplace." The order mandates that the head of each executive agency "shall establish a program to test for the use of illegal drugs by employees in sensitive positions." But the order leaves it up to agency heads to determine "the extent to which such employees are to be tested and the criteria for such testing . . ." The order defines "sensitive position" very broadly, and commentators estimate it could encompass as many as 1.2 million federal employees.

"Drug-Free Federal Workplace" was, not surprisingly, immediately assailed as unconstitutional and unfair by labor unions, civil liberties groups, and some members of Congress. "Reagan has opted

Legal Update

Since the completion of this chapter, three new public workplace decisions have been rendered by federal district courts.

On November 14, 1986, a federal judge sitting in the Eastern District of Louisiana struck down a drug testing program implemented by the United States Customs Service. In a strongly worded opinion, Judge Robert F. Collins held that the program, which subjected all current employees seeking promotions into certain "covered positions" to urinalysis, violated the Fourth Amendment, "penumbral rights of privacy guaranteed by the United States Constitution," and the right to due process of law. The judge concluded, "The plan . . . is so utterly repugnant to the U.S. Constitution, that this Court has no choice but to permanently enjoin Commissioner Von Raab from further implementing it." (National Treasury Employees Union v. Von Raab, U.S. District Court, Eastern District of Louisiana)

Several days later, a federal judge in Tennessee enjoined departmentwide drug testing of fire fighters and police in the City of Chattanooga. The tests, which were to be mandatory and universal, were not conducted pursuant to any written procedures or standards, a fact which deeply troubled Judge Allen Edgar. Judge Edgar ruled that the testing program violated the Fourth Amendment because it was not based on any sort of reasonable suspicion. The judge also observed that

> If indeed the use of drugs is causing deficient performance on the part of fire fighters, this should be detectable to a considerable extent by properly designed personnel procedures to detect such drug abuse symptoms as absenteeism, aberrant conduct and financial difficulties. It does not appear that the City has expended any effort on this approach. (Penny v. Kennedy and Lovvorn v. City of Chattanooga, U.S. District Court for the Eastern District of Tennessee.)

The third decision, announced on December 2, 1985, involved the periodic drug testing of civilian employees (police officers) occupying "critical" positions with the Department of the Army at Ft. Stewart, Georgia. Judge B. Avant Edenfield enjoined the testing program on Fourth Amendment grounds, noting that, ". . . a judicial trend is finally beginning to emerge clearly, and with each new decision on the subject of periodic drug testing it becomes more apparent that testing of civilians by urinalysis, absent some form of individualized suspicion, is in almost all cases offensive to the mandates of the Fourth Amendment." In defending the Army's program, the U.S. Department of Justice asserted that "conditioning public employment on consent to a reasonable drug testing procedure simply puts public-sector employees on the same footing as private-sector employees . . . ." Judge Edenfield considered the government's argument and forcefully rejected it:

> [I]t will be a dark day indeed when the United States government finds it appropriate to abandon the strictures of the Constitution in favor of rules that can allow for infringement of constitutional rights. The Court rejects the government's argument on this point, and sincerely hopes that it will not be advanced in the future. (American Federation of Government Employees, AFL-CIO v. Weinberger, U.S. District Court for the Southern District of Georgia.)

for the role of hangman of federal employees," said the president of the National Treasury Employees Union. "The President's proposal is a blatant violation of the right of American workers to be free of search and seizure without probable cause," the ACLU charged. And Rep. Gary Ackerman (D-New York) accused the President of "suspending" the U.S. Constitution.

The 120,000-member National Treasury Employees Union, which represents employees of the Internal Revenue Service and the U.S. Customs Service, went into federal court without delay on a complaint for declaratory and injunctive relief. "These invasive tests," the complaint alleges, "will be imposed despite the fact that there is no documented problem of drug abuse amongst the federal workplace, without the existence of probable cause, and for a large number of employees without any ground whatsoever to believe they are impaired by, or users of, illegal drugs." Other lawsuits will undoubtedly be brought once agency heads seek to implement the order.

The legal challenges precipitated by President Reagan's order will not be the first time courts have considered the constitutionality of testing public employees for drugs. Numerous decisions have already been rendered by both state and federal judges over the past few years. President Reagan's order may not survive court challenge.

This is the view of the U.S. General Accounting Office, which was asked by the House of Representatives to evaluate a proposed House bill that mandated the testing of federal workers on virtually the same basis as does the Executive Order. In a letter dated September 11, 1986, Comptroller General Charles A. Bowsher surveyed decisional law in the area and declined to support the proposed bill on the grounds that it "raises a constitutional problem and is vague in numerous respects. In addition, the potential benefits are unmeasurable while the estimated costs are significant."

Urinalysis Is a "Search and Seizure" within the Meaning of the Fourth Amendment

The Fourth Amendment to the Constitution, which prohibits "unreasonable searches and seizures by the government," was intended to protect personal privacy and dignity against unwarranted intrusion by the government. Every court that has considered the issue of mandatory urinalysis in the public workplace has held that the test is a search and seizure and that Fourth Amendment standards apply.

When a search of a government employee is conducted for other than law enforcement purposes, as in the case of urinalysis, Fourth Amendment standards do not require that a warrant be obtained. What is involved is the "balancing of the individual's expectation of privacy against the government's right, as an employer, to investigate employee misconduct which is directly relevant to the employee's performance of duties." (Allen v. Marietta) In the majority of cases decided thus far, the courts have held that a public employee can be required to submit to urinalysis only if the employer has "reasonable inferences drawn from those facts in light of experience" that the employee is under the influence of drugs. (McConnell v. Hunter)

Reasonable suspicion can, for example, be based on observation of actual drug use, or on behavior indicating impairment. In Allen v. Marietta, certain employees were observed smoking marijuana at the jobsite. This observation gave the employer the requisite "reasonable suspicion" to justify tests for those employees. In Div. 241, Amalgamated Transit Union v. Suscy, the court upheld the testing of bus drivers who were involved in serious accidents or suspected of being intoxicated on the job.

Random or indiscriminate testing of employees has, with only a few notable exceptions, been found to be unconstitutional. So far federal courts have sustained random or indiscriminate drug testing programs in the military, on the grounds that military personnel have a lesser expectation of privacy than civilians and that the incidence of drug-abuse in the Armed Forces is extensive. (Murray v. Haldeman; Committee for GI Rights v. Callaway.) One federal appeals court also sustained random testing of jockeys on the grounds that horse racing is a unique industry that is subject to "pervasive and continuous state regulation." Shoemaker v. Handel. But note that another court has characterized Shoemaker as "out of step with the rest of the authorities." Caruso v. Ward.

Urinalysis and the Employees Expectation of Privacy

In striking the difficult balance between the employee's expectation of privacy and the public employer's right to investigate the employee misconduct, the courts have been troubled by two features of urine testing: the manner in which specimens are collected, and the examination of one's bodily fluids "for the secrets they may hold."

As noted earlier, in order to insure the chain of custody of a urine sample, it must be collected in the presence of a witness who must actually observe the subject in the act of voiding. A number of judges have commented on this uniquely embarrassing procedure. In Caruso v. Ward, New York State Supreme Court Judge Parness, in throwing out a random testing program directed at members of the Police Department's Organized Crime Bureau, observed:

> Drawing blood is at most a benign procedure. No embarrassment is involved and it is no more invasive or painful than a pin prick...The urine sample must be provided in the presence of a superior officer of the same sex. Thus, the subject officer would be required to perform before another person what is an otherwise very private bodily function which necessarily includes exposing one's private parts, an experience which even if courteously supervised can be humiliating and degrading.

The presence of a witness is now standard practice in methadone clinics. After years of permitting recovering addicts to void in private, it was discovered that many were smuggling "clean" urine, which they had purchased on the outside, into the bathrooms with them.

The subsequent examination and analysis of one's urine also intrudes on the right to privacy. In invalidating the state of Iowa's random testing program for Department of Corrections employees, Federal Judge Vietor stated:

> One does not reasonably expect to discharge urine under circumstances making it available to others to collect and analyze in order to discover the personal physiological secrets it holds except as part of a medical examination. It is significant that both blood and urine can be analyzed in a medical laboratory to discover numerous physiological facts about the person from whom it came, including, but hardly limited to, recent ingestion of alcohol or drugs. One clearly has a reasonable and legitimate expectation of privacy in such personal information contained in his body fluids. (McDonnell v. Hunter.)

On the other side of the equation stands the government employer's right to investigate employee misconduct and insure "the efficiency of the service." Public employers have advanced a number of rationales for instituting urinalysis programs which are based on something *less* than "reasonable suspicion" or "probable cause."

Discovery of Drug Users

Employers have argued that since impairment caused by drug use is often difficult to observe, testing everyone is the only way to find out who the users are. No court has yet accepted that as a valid justification for random testing and several have pointedly rejected it:

> No doubt most employers consider it undesirable for employees to use drugs, and would like to be able to identify any who use drugs. Taking and testing body fluid specimens, as well as conducting searches and seizures of other kinds, would help the employer discover drug use and other useful information about employees. . . There is no doubt about it—searches and seizures can yield a wealth of information useful to the searcher. (That is why King George III's men so frequently searched the colonist.) That potential, however, does not make a governmental employer's search of an employee a constitutionally reasonable one. (McDonnell v. Hunter)

Public Safety

In some cases employers have argued that they should be permitted to test on a random basis when public safety might be in jeopardy. The courts have split on the validity of this rationale. In the New Jersey horse racing case, the court agreed with the State Racing Commission's contention that random testing was necessary in order to maintain safety during the running of a race when most serious accidents occur. Similarly, in the case of Fraternal Order of Police v. Newark, a state court judge upheld the City of Newark's decision to test every police officer for drugs, partially on the basis of the safety rationale: "They are armed; on occasion they use firearms. If even one among the police force were a user, he would be a danger to himself and his fellow police officers."

On the other hand, in the New York City police officers case (Caruso v. Ward), the state court did not accept the safety argument. And in Jones v. McKenzie, in which the plaintiff was a school bus aide, a federal court held that the public safety considerations asserted by the employer were not sufficient to overcome the aide's privacy interest.

Deterrent Effect

In the New York City police officers case, the Police Department sought to persuade the court that random testing would deter drug use among the 1,200 members of the Organized Crime Bureau. The judge rejected this rationale on the ground that the department had not presented proof of a drug problem in the bureau: "Without any direct or even circumstantial proof that a drug problem exists. . .it is difficult to justify random testing as a deterrent when there is little indication that there is any significant drug use to deter." The judge did not indicate if he might have ruled differently had the department proved pervasive drug use among its employees. One of the judicially accepted rationales for random testing in the military was the rampant drug problem in that organization.

Part of the Routine Medical Examination

In the Iowa prison guard case (McDonnell v. Hunter), while the judge invalidated urinalysis that was not based on reasonable suspicion of drug use, he excepted from that principle the giving of a urine specimen as part of a preemployment physical examination or as part of any "routine periodic physical examination that may be required of employees."

But in a New York State case in which a local Board of Education wanted to administer a drug test to all probationary teachers, allegedly as part of a physical examination called for by the collective bargaining agreement, the court found that the teachers had already gone through the medical exam and the subsequent testing called for by the board was investigatory in nature. (Patchogue-Medford Congress of Teachers v. Board of Education.)

And in the Washington, D.C., school bus aide case, the federal court rejected the city's argument that urinalysis was an appropriate incident of the annual physical examination and ruled that testing could only be done on the basis of probable cause. (Jones v. McKenzie)

Consent

A couple of courts have dealt with the issue of "voluntary consent" to urinalysis and have held that even written consent did not constitute a waiver of legitimate privacy rights. Basing his decision on a U.S. Supreme Court case which ruled that public employees cannot be bound by unreasonable conditions of employment, the federal judge in the Iowa prison guard case held that "Advance consent to future *unreasonable* searches is not a reasonable condition of employment." The ruling in the New York police case was the same.

Drug Testing and Due Process

In the early morning hours of May 26, 1986, the Fire Chief of Plainfield, New Jersey, and the city's Director of Public Affairs and Safety entered the city fire station, secured and locked all the doors, awakened the fire fighters then present in the firehouse, and required each and every one of them to provide a urine sample while under the surveillance and supervision of bonded testing agents. The fire-fighters had not been forewarned that they were going to be tested, and the testing was not done pursuant to any witten policy. Sixteen men were subsequently advised their test results were positive and were termi-nated without pay. They were not informed of which drug had been found in their urine. No confirmatory tests were performed. Nor were they given an opportunity to contest the results at a hearing. Ten days later they were served with written complaints charging each of them with the "commission of a criminal act."

The firefighters went into federal court, complaining that their constitutional rights had been violated, and on September 18, 1986, Federal Judge H. Lee Sarokin handed down a strongly worded decision finding that the "raid" constituted an unreasonable search and seizure in violation of the Fourth Amendment, and condemning Plainfield's "flagrant violation of the due process rights" of the firemen. He ordered the sixteen reinstated.

It has long been established by the courts that public employees have a "property interest" in their continued employment. This interest, protected by the Fourteenth Amendment of the Constitution, entitles them to procedural due process before they can be terminated.

The City of Plainfield did not observe even the most minimal procedural safeguards: the right to be notified in advance of a new condition of employment, the right to object, the right to written policy, the right to confidentiality, the right to review the test results, and the right to a pretermination hearing. The judge was appalled:

> The harassment, coercion and tactics utilized here, even if motivated by the best of intentions, should cause us all to recognize the realities of government excesses and the need for constant vigilance against intrusions into constitutional rights by its agents. If we choose to violate the rights of the innocent in order to discover and act against the guilty, then we will have transformed our country into a police state and abandon one of the fundamental tenets of our free society. In order to win the war against drugs, we must not sacrifice the life of the Constitution in the battle.
>
> Capuba v. Plainfield

In summary, in the public employment arena the courts have, with very few exceptions, rejected urinalysis programs that are not based on some kind of individualized suspicion. In doing so, drug testing has been firmly linked to impaired job performance or observation of actual drug use on the job. Judges, both state and federal, have almost uniformly found testing programs that subject many innocent people to urinalysis in order to find the guilty few repugnant to notions of privacy and fairness. They are also concerned that the testing and the personnel decisions which flow from a positive result comport with well-established due process requirements.

We will definitely see more public employment decisions in the months to come. President Reagan's Executive Order, which has already been challenged by one labor union, will come under further legal attack. The City of Glendale in southern California was recently sued by the ACLU for requiring all city employees desirous of a promotion to undergo urinalysis. Some of the decisions discussed herein have been appealed and will soon be ruled upon by higher courts. But there is no reason to believe that the judicial trend against random drug testing will be reversed in the future.

III. DRUG TESTING IN THE PRIVATE WORKPLACE

Because the constitutional protection against unreasonable searches and seizures constrains only the actions of public employers, the law of drug testing in the private sector is evolving with different dynamics. At the time of this writing, only a handful of individual employees and unions have filed lawsuits against private employers. Inevitably, more will be brought. Civil liberties groups are actively looking for test cases to bring, and labor unions are developing legal strategies to protect their members from what they regard as unwarranted and unfair drug tests. (Consider, for example the November 10, 1986, conference entitled "The Drug Testing Debate: Remedy or Reaction?", held in Washington, D.C., and co-sponsored by the American Civil Liberties Union and the AFL-CIO. The conference stated its goal as "constructing legal, legislative and workplace-based alternatives to unrestricted drug testing.")

There is already a well-developed body of arbitration decisions pertaining to drug abuse and drug testing that unionized companies must consider before implementing a testing program. And although court decisions are still sparse, it is possible to discern broad trends that may protect nonunionized employees and even job applicants from drug testing.

All of these trends and developments must be seen against the backdrop of the gradual erosion of the employment-at-will doctrine. The employment-at-will doctrine was an American invention, a product of the laissez-faire political economy of the nineteenth century. Simply stated, employment-at-will meant that an employer could discharge an employee "for good cause, for no cause or even for a cause morally wrong." (Payne v. Western & Alt. RR, 81 Tenn. 507. 1884). This was a departure from English common law, which as far back as 1562 placed limits upon the power of an employer to terminate an employee unless there was reasonable cause to do so.

The employment-at-will doctrine held sway in America until the early 1930s, when the harsh economic realities of the Great Depression led to massive legislative action. Recognition of employees' rights to organize and bargain collectively for higher wages and better working conditions led to a radical realignment of power in those workplaces that were unionized. Civil rights laws followed in the 1960s and 70s, making further inroads on the employer's previously unfettered power to hire and fire at will.

One commentator has stated that "the employment-at-will issue is well on its way to becoming the labor law issue of the 80s." (Kenneth Lopatka, "The Emerging Law of Wrongful Discharge—A Quadrennial Assessment of the Labor Law Issue of the 80s," 40 Business Lawyer 1 (1984)). In the past five years, a majority of state courts have recognized a variety of new exceptions to the employment-at-will doctrine, and these exceptions may provide legal handles to employees who are discharged on the basis of their refusal to submit to a drug test or the results of a test taken.

Another piece of the backdrop having major implications for the future of employee drug testing is the gradual expansion of the "right to privacy" in American jurisprudence. Increasing judicial sensitivity to "zones of privacy" can be traced back to the Supreme Court's historic decision in Griswold v. Connecticut (381 U.S. 479, 1965). In that case, an anticontraception state statute was voided as an infringment of the "right to marital privacy." Although privacy is nowhere mentioned in the Bill of Rights, the court found it in the "penumbras" of other guarantees and in the language of the seldom used Ninth Amendment: "The enumeration in the Constitution, of certain rights, shall not be construed to deny or disparage others retained by the people."

Since 1965, literally hundreds of privacy laws have been passed by Congress and state legislatures, and a number of states have amended their constitutions to include an explicit right to privacy.

Exceptions to the employment-at-will doctrine combined with notions of privacy will provide the conceptual framework for anti-drug-testing litigation in the future. But first let's examine trends in the unionized workplace.

Drug Testing in the Unionized Workplace

Unionized companies attempting unilaterally to implement drug testing programs are more than likely to encounter strong opposition from the union. While many unions are concerned about drug and alcohol abuse among their members, they bridle at the unilateral imposition of new rules by management and at testing programs which are not based on cause. In May of 1986, the AFL-CIO Executive Council adopted a policy on "Mandatory Drug and Alcohol Tests," which states in part:

We deplore the recent efforts by many employers, in the hysteria of the moment, to bypass the collective bargaining process and require mandatory screening or impose punitive programs which ride roughshod over the rights and dignity of workers and are unnecessary to secure a safe and efficient workforce.

The AFL-CIO urges its affiliates to vigorously resist these harsh and unjustifiable programs and to assist union members who are injured by such employer-imposed programs to invoke their rights under federal and state law.

The AFL-CIO's concerns have, to an extent, struck a responsive chord with arbitrators and the courts.

1. Bypassing the collective bargaining process.

The National Labor Relations Law (NLRA) makes it an unfair labor practice for an employer to refuse to bargain collectively over terms and conditions of employment. Rules regarding employee conduct and the imposition of discipline for breaches of those rules are mandatory subjects of bargaining. Attempts unilaterally to impose mandatory, random testing programs on current employees have been successfully challenged by unions.

In International Brotherhood of Electrical Workers, Local 1900 v. Potomac Electric Power Co. (D.C.D.C. 1986), the company had sought to implement new drug and alcohol rules that were much more severe than its previous rules. The new rules provided for immediate discharge for refusal to submit to a blood or urine test or a locker, lunchbox or personal search, and for the presence of any detectable quantity of drugs in one's system. They also dispensed with the company's previous practice of subjecting positive test results to confirmatory testing. The union applied for a temporary restraining order against the implementation of the new rules pending arbitration. The federal judge granted the order with the following observation:

> In my opinion the plaintiff [union] is likely to prevail on the merits of this lawsuit, at least in the sense that the draconian measures which the defendant [company] has proposed and perhaps implemented cannot be unilaterally imposed under the law without exhaustion of some procedures under the collective bargaining agreement and particularly arbitration.

In a similar case, Brooklyn Union Gas Co. was temporarily restrained from adding drug testing to the annual physical examinations of all employees, pending arbitration of the union's objections. (Local 101, Utility Division, Transport Workers Union of America v. Brooklyn Union Gas Co., N.Y. Sup. Ct. 1986.)

And in a case brought by the Brotherhood of Maintenance of Way Employees against Burlington Northern Railroad Co., the U.S. Court of Appeals for the 8th Circuit ruled, on October 1, 1986, that under the terms of the Railway Labor Act the company could implement an expanded version of its drug testing program, but that it had to engage in settlement of the dispute through arbitration.

It is, therefore, clear that the imposition of a program for periodic and/or random drug testing is arbitrable and that it would be prudent to consult with the union prior to its implementation.

2. Challenges to disciplinary actions based upon drug use or abuse.

Even after a drug testing program is in place, there may be union grievances filed regarding individual employees who have been disciplined on the basis of a positive test. In general, arbitrators are reluctant to sustain discharges based on drug-related conduct. One commentator recently conducted a survey of arbitration decisions reported in the Labor Arbitration Reports between March 1980 and January 1985 and discovered that drug-related discharges were sustained in only 21 of 46 cases (excluding those involving actual sale of drugs). He posits that it is difficult for unionized employers to sustain disciplinary action because, in drug cases, arbitrators hold them to a higher standard of proof than is normally the case (e.g., "beyond reasonable doubt" or "clear and convincing evidence," rather than the less stringent "preponderance of the evidence" standard). ("Drug and Alcohol Abuse In the Workplace: Balancing Employer and Employee Rights", Thomas E. Geidt, II *Employee Relations Law Journal* 181 (1985-86)). Employers who opt for a punitive rather than rehabilitative model for dealing with drug use or abuse should be aware that their union may grieve any disciplinary measures taken and that the union stands a better than 50 percent chance of winning in arbitration.

3. Drug testing arbitrations in the transportation industry.

The transportation industry was a maverick in the use of urinalysis to detect drug use among its employees. Greyhound began using the EMIT test in early 1982 on urine samples collected from employees during periodic physical examinations. A positive EMIT test resulted in discharge. The arbitration decisions rendered in several of the discharge cases are illustrative of the range of problems arbitrators have with disciplinary measures based on drug tests. And the early Greyhound experience may serve as a useful negative example for companies contemplating drug testing.

Case Study #1

In Amalgamated Transit Union, Div. No. 1225 and Greyhound Lines, Inc. (San Francisco), five employees were discharged solely on the basis of the results of EMIT tests administered as part of physical examinations just months after the company initiated its testing program. In all five cases, the test was positive for marijuana. Arbitrator Thomas Knowlton held that the discharges were not for sufficient cause and reinstated all five grievants contingent upon their passing a new EMIT test.

While the arbitrator acknowledged the company's right to utilize the EMIT test and take disciplinary action on the basis of test results, he was troubled by the fact that "the EMIT Assays were included in the physical examinations of the grievants without any notice to the Union or the employees." He reinstated the employees because they had never been notified that off-duty use of marijuana constituted a violation of the work rules.

Case Study #2

In Amalgamated Transit Union, Div. 1202 and Greyhound Lines, Inc. (New York City), the grievant was discharged after three of his urine specimens, taken on three separate days, were positive for marijuana, and in the case of one specimen, cocaine. Arbitrator Arvid Anderson reinstated the grievant on the condition that he pass a new drug test.

As in the first case study, Arbitrator Anderson was troubled by the fact that the company had never informed the union or its employees that it was subjecting urine samples to drug tests and that employees would be disciplined for off-duty drug use.

The arbitrator also rejected the company's argument that marijuana use should be treated differently from alcohol use because the former substance is illegal:

> The abuse of either alcohol or the use of narcotics is obviously a danger to safe job performance, which is the real reason for the Rule 16 [prohibiting drug or alcohol use on company premises and the use of narcotics at all times], not its illegality. The fact that employees may be guilty of criminal activity including the use or possession of narcotics does not per se mean that they are subject to discharge. There is the necessity of showing that such criminal activity is in some way job related. None has been shown in this case.

Finally, the arbitrator noted that the company produced no evidence that the grievant "performed his duties in a manner which showed that he was under the influence of narcotics." While condemning the use of narcotics, he indicated that "where there is no evidence that such use has in any way affected their job performance," there may not be cause for discharge.

Case Study #3

Local 656, United Automobile, Aerospace and Agricultural Implement Workers of America (UAW) and Greyhound Lines, Inc. (Detroit) was decided in October, 1985. By this time the company's policy regarding off-duty drug use had been clearly publicized to all employees, and evidently the company was subjecting positive drug screens to confirmatory testing by GC/MS, thereby eliminating most false positives. Nevertheless, the grievant in this case, who had tested positive for marijuana during a bi-annual physical examination, was reinstated with full back pay, benefits, and seniority.

In this case the union launched a full-scale attack on the work rule prohibiting drug use "at all times," arguing that the rule could not be invoked without a showing that the employee's work performance was impaired. In reviewing the considerable evidence presented by the union and the company, Arbitrator Alan Walt adopted the well-settled arbitral position that "a rule which regulated off-duty conduct must bear a reasonable relationship to the employer's operations" and found "a total absence of evidence establishing *any* relationship between the presence of marijuana in grievant's urine and the company's operations, including such relevant factors as safety, efficiency, and productivity."

Arbitrator Walt noted that since marijuana remains in the system for up to 50 days after ingestion, "there is a need for evidence which will establish the length of time over which the presence of marijuana in the urine can have a physical, psychological, or psychophysiological effect on an individual." Without such reputable scientific evidence, a showing of the presence of the marijuana metabolite in urine "does not establish the needed nexus to the employment relationship."

Since there is no current, scientifically accepted measure of impairment from marijuana ingestion (as there is in the case of alcohol), this arbitration decision stands for the proposition that disciplinary action is based on off-duty drug use as indicated by a positive urine test will be upheld only if it is linked to impaired job performance.

In summary, then, unionized companies that are planning to implement drug testing programs would be wise, at a minimum, to:

1. Inform the union and negotiate any disagreements as to the terms of the program;
2. Publicize the policy clearly to all employees, including the consequences of a positive test result;
3. Confirm positive drug screens with a different type of urine test; and
4. Impose disciplinary action only where there is evidence of imparied job performance or actual on-duty use.

This last point raises the fundamental issue of whether it ever makes sense to subject unionized employees to drug testing in the absence of just cause.

LAWS PROHIBITING DISCRIMINATION BASED ON HANDICAP

The Rehabilitation Act (29 U.S.C. §701 et seq.), passed by Congress in 1973, prohibits the federal government, federal contractors, and employers receiving any form of federal financial assistance from discriminating against qualified handicapped persons:

§504. No otherwise qualified handicapped individual in the United States...shall, solely by reason of his handicap, be excluded from the participation in, be denied the benefits of, or be subject to discrimination under any program or activity receiving Federal financial assistance.

A handicapped individual is described in §706 (6) as:
[A]ny person...who (a) has a physical or mental impairment which substantially limits one or more of such person's major life activities, (b) has a record of such impairment, or (c) is regarded as having such an impairment.

In the first few years following the law's enactment, there was some controversy over whether alcoholism and drug addiction were "handicaps" under the Act. This confusion was cleared up definitively in 1977 when the Department of Health, Education and Welfare (HEW) issued its analysis of several sections of the Act (at 42 Fed.Reg. 22686, 5/4/77). According to the Department's analysis, drug addiction and alcoholism are "physical and mental impairments" and are therefore handicaps for purposes of the Rehabilitation Act. Furthermore, section 504 of the Act covers "persons who have been incorrectly classified as having" a handicap. And finally, the Act does not protect individuals whose handicap, including alcoholism or drug addiction, "prevents successful performance on the job."

Since the publication of HEW's analysis, several cases have been decided in favor of protection for drug and alcohol abusers. In one case, a federal court held that the City of Philadelphia's blanket ban on hiring current and/or former drug abusers violated the Act (Davis v. Bucher, 451 F.Supp. 791, E.D.Pa. 1978). In another, a college that refused to grant tenure to a professor who had revealed his alcoholism was found to have violated the Act (Whitaker v. Board of Higher

Education of the City of New York, 461 F.Supp. 99 E.D.N.Y. 1978).

The language, legislative history, and administrative and judicial interpretations of The Rehabilitation Act strongly suggest that current and former drug abusers, *and* those "regarded" as being such, who are otherwise able to perform their jobs, cannot lawfully be discriminated against by any employer who receives some form of federal financial assistance.

Even a job applicant who denies having a drug problem could be covered by the Act since it also protects those mistakenly "regarded" as having a handicap. And obviously the employer would not be in the position to defend the decision not to hire on the basis of impaired job performance.

Most of the states have also passed laws prohibiting discrimination on the basis of handicap in both public and private employment. While few cases have been brought under these statutes thus far, many of them closely track the federal act's language and may well be found to cover drug abusers or those incorrectly perceived to be drug abusers.

These federal and state laws may have major implications for workplace drug testing, particularly in the realm of preemployment screening. If a job applicant who is in all other respects qualified is turned down solely on the basis of a positive drug test, (s)he may very well have a valid claim under the Federal Rehabilitation Act or a comparable state law. The employer's presumption is that a positive test result indicates a drug abuse problem, i.e., a "handicap" under the Act. Even a job applicant who denies having a drug problem could, conceivably, be "regarded" as having a handicap. [Again, the employer would need to defend his position on the basis of impaired job performance.]

The Act may also protect current employees with real or mistakenly perceived drug abuse problems from any adverse actions, such as discharge or denial of promotion, unless the employer can show some impairment of the employee's job performance.

This is an area to watch closely. It is only a matter of time before applicants and employees who have suffered the consequences of a positive drug test will begin filing federal and state claims under the appropriate discrimination laws.

There are, of course, job categories for which use and/or abuse, even if considered as a handicap, would result in disqualification. Various actions have upheld a public sector employer's denial of employment when public safety (e.g., driving a bus) was at issue. Although the Act was not evoked in these decisions, the principle is established.

SUITS FOR WRONGFUL DISCHARGE

The "wrongful discharge" suit represents a direct challenge to the employment-at-will doctrine. A relatively contemporary legal animal, it may turn out to be the employee-at-will's equivalent to a union contract. Employees who are discharged for refusing to take or for failing a drug test that was not based on cause may find in the wrongful discharge action a vehicle for vindicating what they perceive to be their right to continued employment.

Three-fifths of the states now recognize a cause of action for wrongful discharge in one form or another (Lopatka, ibid). Moreover jury awards for prevailing employees in such cases tend to be quite substantial. Two California studies completed in 1983 showed a 90 to 95 percent plantiff success rate and a $450,000-$548,000 median damage award for wrongful discharge suits in that state, and warns that "the California verdicts may be a harbinger of things to come elsewhere."

Although the law of wrongful discharge is in its infancy and state courts are far from unanimous in its application (the New York State Court of Appeals, for example, has refused to recognize wrongful discharge on the grounds that it is the state legislature's function to create so broad an exception to employment-at-will. (Murphy v. American Home Products Corp., 461 N.Y.S.2d 232, 1983), employers ought to consider its implications before subjecting the current employee whose job performance is satisfactory to drug testing leading to discharge.

The courts that have recognized wrongful discharge have grounded their holdings on two basic theories: public policy and implied contract.

Discharge in Violation of Public Policy

In the words of one of the increasing number of courts that have ruled on this issue, "where a clear mandate of public policy is violated by the employee's termination, the employer's right to discharge may be circumscribed (Reuther v. Fowler & Williams, Inc., 255 Pa.Super. 28, 1978). Courts in at least 22 states have recognized an exception to employment-at-will on public policy grounds. Where there is no clear formula for determining whether a discharge violates public policy in a particular jurisdiction, successful lawsuits fall into several distinct categories.

The first involves cases where employees were terminated for refusing to commit wrongful act such as perjury, before a legislative committee (Peterman v. International Brotherhood of Teamsters Local 396, 174 Cal. App. 2nd 184, 1959).

The second category includes cases in which an employee was fired for performing a public obligation such as serving on a jury (Nees v. Hocks, 272 Or.210, 1975).

Finally, a third category of cases involves discharges based on an employee's exercise of certain legal rights. It is this category of cases that may have some bearing on employee drug testing. If drug tests were found to contravene public policy, then an employee who exercised his right to refuse to submit to a drug test might be able to successfully fight his consequent discharge. And since discharge in violation of a public policy is a tort, a wronged employee could be awarded punitive as well as actual damages.

Pennsylvania has probably gone further than any other state in recognizing "tortious discharge in violation of public policy." In 1979 a case involving a discharged employee-at-will who alleged he had been fired for refusing to take a polygraph examination, the federal Court of Appeals for the Third Circuit held that such a discharge violated the public policy of Pennsylvania (Perks v. Firestone Tire and Rubber Co., 611 F.2nd 1363, 1978). The court based its decision on a state statute prohibiting employers from requiring employees to take polygraph tests as a condition of employment.

In Novosel v. Nationwide Ins. Co. (721 F.2d 894, 1983) the same court held that a Pennsylvania salesman who had been fired for refusing to participate in his employer's lobbying efforts because he disagreed with the employer's legislative agenda, had been discharged in violation of public policy. Significantly, the court held that " a cognizable expression of public policy can be derived in this case from either the First Amendment to the U.S. Constitution or Art. I, Sec. 7 of the Pennsylvania Constitution" ("The free communication of thoughts and opinions is one of the invaluable rights of man. . .") In

On December 16, 1986 a suit was filed in Massachusettes Superior Court by the ACLU against the Liquid Carbonic Corp. on behalf of an employee who was discharged on the basis of one positive, random urine test. The complaint charges that the discharge "was contrary to public policy and therefore constituted a wrongful termination in violation of Massachusetts tort law." The plaintiff prays for reinstatement, and injunction prohibiting further testing, and damages in the amount of $74,000 plus attorney's fees. (Jackson v. Liquid Carbonic Corp.)

applying the values embodied in the Constitution to a private employment relationship, the court argued:

> The protection of important political freedoms goes well beyond the question whether the threat comes from state or private bodies. The inquiry before us is whether the concern for the rights of political expression and association which animate the public employee cases is sufficient to state a public policy under Pennsylvania law.

The court's answer was affirmative.

The reasoning found in the Novosel case could be applied to random drug testing by an adventuresome court. A "cognizable expression of public policy" could be found in the Fourth Amendment or equivalent state constitutional provisions. As in the Novosel opinion, a survey of public employee cases would demonstrate the judiciary's concern for the protected privacy rights which are violated by random drug tests. Ergo, discharge for refusal to submit to such a drug test violates an important public policy.

Breach of Implied Employment Contract

The vast majority of nonunionized employees do not have written employment contracts. But, increasingly, courts have been willing to find implied contracts under a variety of circumstances. To date, courts in about 20 states have recognized wrongful discharge actions based on breach of implied employment contracts (including

Alabama, Alaska, Arizona, California, Idaho, Kentucky, Maine, Massachusetts, Michigan, Minnesota, Missouri, Nevada, New Mexico, New York, Oklahoma, Oregon, South Dakota, and Washington).

Implied contracts have been found in oral statements, employee handbooks and even job applications. For example, in the case of Toussaint v. Blue Cross & Blue Shield (408 Mich. 579, 1980), which is considered to be one of the most far-reaching of these decisions, the Michigan Supreme Court found an implied contract of employment in an employee handbook which contained language to the effect that it was the company's policy "to provide for the administration of fair, consistent and reasonable corrective discipline" and "to release employees for just cause only." The court upheld a jury verdict that the employee could only be discharged for just cause.

Even in the absence of an employee handbook, job application, or oral representation, some courts have nevertheless found contractual rights flowing from the "covenant of good faith and fair dealing." This view holds that every employment agreement implicitly requires the parties to deal with each other fairly and in good faith. Employers may breach this duty if they treat an employee unfairly or discharge the employee arbitrarily or without good cause.

The Supreme Court of New Hampshire adopted a very expansive construction of the implied covenant of good faith and fair dealing in the case of Monge v. Beebe Rubber Co. (316 A.2d 549, 1974). There, a woman employee was fired when she rejected her supervisor's sexual advances. The court held that "a termination by the employer of a contract of employment at will which is motivated by bad faith or malice or based on retaliation is not in the best interest of the economic system or the public good and constitutes a breach of the employment contract." The California courts have also held that the covenant of good faith and fair dealing may prohibit an employer from terminating a long-term employee without good cause (e.g., Cleary v. American Airlines, Inc., 168 Cal.Rptr. 722, 1980).

Although no court decisions have yet been rendered on drug testing and wrongful discharge, a number of cases are now pending against private companies which raise the issue. Several of these were brought by the American Civil Liberties Union.

In one case, a California company subjected a group of oil refinery workers to random drug testing. Refusal to comply with a company request for a urine sample, or failure of a screening test, results in automatic discharge. (Price v. Pacific Refinery Co., pending

74

before Superior Ct., State of California, Contra Costa County). A-nother case involves 11 workers from a lumber company in Washington who were discharged based on the results of one unconfirmed drug test. The employees were told by management that the quality of their work was not a factor in their terminations. (Sutton v. Olympic Forest Products, Inc., pending before Superior Ct., State of Washington, Thurston Co.). In both cases, the employees are alleging, among numerous other grounds, that their discharges were wrongful based on both violation of public policy and breach of implied contract.

Violation of the Right to Privacy

The right "to be let alone," which Supreme Court Justice Louis Brandeis once called "the most comprehensive of rights and the right most valued by civilized men," derives from a number of sources: from common law, from state constitutional provisions and from state statutes addressing such specific concerns as the confidentiality of various kinds of records, the use of polygraphing in employment, and the electronic gathering of information by cable television. Every technological advance that implicates privacy seems to occasion a response from the courts and eventually the enactment of protective legislation.

The Common Law Right to Privacy.

The laws of virtually every state recognize the common law right to privacy, which has traditionally applied to four different forms of encroachment: (1) intrusion upon solitude, (2) public disclosure of private facts, (3) casting one in a false light, and (4) use of one's name or image for another person's profit. Since the invasion of privacy is an action in tort, a prevailing plaintiff is entitled not only to actual, but to punitive or exemplary damages as well.

A 1984 case from Texas is worth looking at. In K-Mart v. Trotti (677 S.W.2d 636, Tx. Ct. of Appeals, 1984) an employee sued her employer for invasion of privacy because her locker and personal effects had been searched, even though she was not actually suspected of any wrongdoing. The court noted that "mere suspicion either that another employee had stolen watches, or that unidentified employees may have stolen price-marking guns was insufficient to justify the search of the plaintiff's locker and possessions" and ruled that the search constituted an invasion of privacy, which it defined as "an intentional intrusion upon the solitude or seclusion of another that is highly offensive to a reasonable person." Furthermore, the court upheld the employee's related claim that the search had caused her mental anguish, defined as follows:

> The term "mental anguish" implies a relatively high degree of distress. It is more than mere disappointment, anger, resentment, or embarrassment, although it may include all of these. It includes a mental sensation of pain resulting from such painful emotion as grief, severe disappointment, indignation, wounded pride, shame, despair and/or public humiliation.

And finally, the court upheld the jury's award of exemplary damages on the ground that "exemplary damages exist to promote the protection of an important public interest by making an example of the defendant for particular wrongful, malicious conduct." The award totaled $108,000.

It would appear that the K-Mart court's reasoning could be applied with equal force to drug tests that are not based on cause. And it is a cause of action which anyone who has unwillingly submitted to urinalysis could theoretically initiate, job applicants and current employees alike.

In December 1986 the ACLU initiated a class action suit against Minco Technology Labs Inc., a Texas corporation, which last September announced a new drug testing policy. The policy would subject all current employees "to routine, periodic urinalysis drug testing." The suit seeks to prohibit the company's implementation of the policy on the ground it violates the right to privacy under Texas common law.

State Constitutions and the Right to Privacy.

Nine states have in their constitutions explicit right to privacy language: Alaska, Arizona, California, Hawaii, Illinois, Louisiana,

Montana, South Carolina, and Washington. There is not yet a great deal of case law interpreting these constitutional provisions and it is not clear that all of them apply to private as well as state actions. But the right to privacy under the California constitution does apply to private action and a number of drug testing suits are currently pending in that state. The suits are principally based on state constitutional grounds.

In 1972 the voters of California amended article I, section I of the state constitution to add privacy to a series of "inalienable rights." The amendment's legislative history expresses great concern over increased surveillance and data collection activity in contemporary society, and states, "At present there are no effective restraints on the informational activities of government and business. This amendment creates a legal and enforceable right of privacy for every Californian."

The legal complaint filed on behalf of the employee of Pacific Refining Company (see p. 74) cites ten distinct ways in which the company's universal drug testing policy violates the right to privacy guaranteed by the California constitution. The litany of violations demonstrates the potential breadth of the constitution's premise:

a. Requiring employees to undergo drug testing as a condition of continued employment;
b. Mandating the termination of employees who undergo drug testing and whose test results are positive;
c. Requiring employees to execute authorizations for the release of confidential medical information to Pacific, its agents, servants and employees.
d. Implementing procedures for drug testing which require employees to expose private parts of their bodies to lab technicians while giving a urine sample;
e. Requiring employees to provide bodily fluids;
f. Reporting the results of employees' drug tests to persons and entities not expressly authorized to receive the results;
g. Holding up employees' drug test results to the possible scorn of co-workers, supervisors, potential employers, and others;
h. Attempting to direct and control off-duty conduct of employees;
i. Attempting to direct and control the off-duty conduct of employees when there is no reasonable ground to believe that their faculties and job performance are impaired; and

j. Intruding into the off-duty conduct of the lives of employees without a compelling need to do so.

There are also two major cases pending against Southern Pacific Transportation Co., which instituted a random testing program in 1985. In one case (Luck v. Southern Pacific) the employee was discharged for refusing to submit to a drug test. In the second case (Pettigrew v. Southern Pacific), the employee was confined for 28 days in a hospital treatment program even though his second drug test was negative (his first was positive for cocaine, but he had taken a non-prescription allergy medication that day) and the physicians at the hospital found no evidence to confirm any suspicion of chemical dependency. Both employees have requested jury trials and are asking for millions of dollars in damages.

State and Local Laws

In December of 1985, the San Francisco Board of Supervisors passed an ordinance which prohibits most drug testing by private industry in that city. This event made San Francisco the only jurisdiction in the country with protective legislation pertaining to drug testing—a uniqueness it still enjoys.

The ordinance, which is grounded in the state constitution's right to privacy, has the stated purpose of protecting "employees against unreasonable inquiry and investigation into off-the-job conduct, associations, and activities not directly related to the actual performance of job responsibilities." It permits drug testing only if the employer has "reasonable grounds to believe an employee's faculties are impaired on the job, and the employee is in a position where such impairment presents a clear and present danger to the physical safety of the employee, another employee or a member of the public." The ordinance exempts from its coverage "emergency services personnel" and job applicants. No cases have yet been brought under the ordinance.

Statutes protecting the confidentiality of medical records may also implicate aspects of drug testing. Rhode Island, for example, has a statute requiring organizations that keep medical information to adopt policies to assure confidentiality. Massachusetts passed a Patient's Bill of Rights in 1979 which confers a right to "con-

78

fidentiality of all records and communication to the extent provided by law."

Employers must be very careful in implementing drug testing programs, that they not run afoul of applicable confidentiality laws in terms of who has access to the laboratory test reports or results, to what extent employees or applicants are required to divulge information on legal drugs and medications they are taking, and what is ultimately done with the test results.

CONCLUSION

Drug testing raises complex legal questions. An organization contemplating any sort of testing should seek the advice of corporate counsel.

But do not expect a definitive answer. Many drug testing practices are currently under legal challenge. Until decisions are handed down and appeals are exhausted, testing will be fraught with potential liabilities.

Conservative measures are less likely to prove litigious. Testing for cause, with the promise of rehabilitative services rather than the threat of termination, seems the path of least legal resistance.

Testing that does not directly relate to job impairment—that is to say, random or universal testing—is at the center of virtually every test case currently pending. The gains realized from such testing are probably unmeasurable; the losses, unpredictable.

AMA research for this report found that half the questionnaire respondents have yet to take a stance on the issue of testing. From a legal standpoint, this policy of "watchful waiting" is the safest course.

3

Drug Education
and Awareness

THE MOST famous vehicle of its time designed to raise public awareness on the dangers of drug abuse was, within thirty years, a laughingstock.

This was _Reefer Madness,_ a feature film released in 1936 to warn America's youth against the insidious effects of marijuana. The drama was, to put it kindly, overplayed. At the puff of a home-rolled joint, teen innocents were transformed into lunatic and lustful beasts for whom sex and violence were mere diversions.

A later generation, which had taken marijuana as its "recreational drug of choice," enjoyed viewing the film at midnight screenings while high on the very substance that played the villian on the screen. The later audience knew from personal experience or direct observation that the immediate effects of marijuana were far less vibrant or threatening. The film's dramatic overstatement had transformed the cautionary tale of the '30's into the farce of the '60's.

Current drug awareness materials must deal with the same challenge to credibility. Statements on the effects of illegal substances, by whatever medium, owe the reader or viewer more respect. But according to several respondents to AMA's questionnaire, some new products might well be titled _Sons of Reefer Madness._ "Carrie Nation with a new cause," said one, reminded of the ax-wielding nineteenth-century temperance reformer.

THE FILMS FROM CORONET/MTI

But other tools currently on the market boast a greater sensitivity to both the facts and the audience. When we asked our respondents to recommend materials they'd found effective in their own drug awareness campaigns, two films distributed by the Chicago-based firm of Coronet/MTI were by far the most frequently cited. Both half-hour docudramas picture drug problems that impact upon co-workers and supervisors as well as users.

Everything Looks So Normal covers a range of problems that affect a large manufacturing/shipping worksite. Managers know that productivity is a problem, but cannot bring themselves to think that substance abuse is at the root—"everything looks so normal." Normality includes executives who pop "uppers," secretaries who trade perscription drugs, managers who snort cocaine in the parking lot, blue-collar workers who both sell and smoke marijuana in the lavoratories. True to life, not every story has a happy ending. One equipment driver (under threat of firing) opts for enrollment in an employee assistance program, but others meet a less happy fate.

The intention is to combat the frequent assumption that "it can't happen here." Managers and supervisors who view the film are brought face to face with patterns of behavior—tardiness, absenteeism, erratic shifts of mood—which may well be symptoms of drug abuse. Solutions are secondary; awareness comes first.

The partner piece, *Whose Problem Is It?*, takes a portion of the first film's focus and makes it central. A shop-floor equipment handler is a heavy user of marijuana. Though his co-workers know of this and urge him against the drug, they cover for his absences and suffer from his mistakes. A brush with a serious accident brings matters to a head; the supervisor takes control, and—again under threat of dismissal—the abuser enters an assistance program.

The film recognizes the natural inclination among workers to protect a member of the team, but suggests that one man's drug abuse is a threat to that team as well as the wider organization. It avoids the moral dilemma of "squealing on a buddy," and instead poses the separate question of the effect of individual behavior upon one's co-workers.

There are certain "givens" in both films. One is the presence of an employee assistance program; another is that corporate management and union officials are united in addressing workplace drug abuse ("The union is with us on this one," a supervisor assures a worker who threatens a grievance if fired for substance abuse). In the cases shown, the films also suppose that treatment for substance abuse is a matter of *choice*. The scripts are free of the words "addict" or "dependency," and the behavior on screen has none of the maddened animal to it. These films are a long way from *Reefer Madness*.

THE NAWGA GUIDE

Like drug testing, awareness efforts function best when they are part of a coordinated program that addresses workplace drug abuse in its totality. It does little good to gather the workforce for a screening of *Whose Problem Is It?* if the film's given elements—rehabilitation services, union support—are not present. Combatting workplace drug abuse requires far more than film and video. It requires a policy.

The National-American Wholesale Grocers' Assocation (NAWGA) offers to its 500 members a model substance abuse program which provides step-by-step information on creating and implementing a working policy. The NAWGA package also uses a video presentation, less dramatic than the Coronet offerings but truer to life; and it surrounds the video with a "how-to" guide for management and a collection of printed materials to distribute to employees.

Based on research compiled by the National Institute for Drug Abuse (NIDA), the NAWGA guide offers a strategy for combating substance abuse and provides samples of policy language and employee notices.

A discussion of the costs and hazards of substance abuse leads to a list of goals the company may wish to achieve with a program. The stress is on the formulation of a task force, involving human resources, medical, and security personnel, as well as legal counsel and representatives from employee groups.

A chapter introduces the reader to the most commonly abused substances, along with descriptions of the symptoms and effects of their use. There follows a thorough review of the methods of drug testing, including examples of the types of tests and the correct protocol for specimen collection. This section emphasizes the importance of selecting a competent laboratory, as false results may soar when proper procedures are neglected, resulting in increased costs for retesting and, often, in legal challenges. The section ends with a review of security measures beyond urine testing: polygraph examinations, electronic surveillance, and use of undercover agents.

From there, the guide looks at employee assistance programs: structures, staffing issues, policies and procedures, employee trust and confidentiality of records and results. Next is an overview of employee relations, and the tricky question of informing workers about a company's concern about drug use without alienating or offending the workforce: by communicating policy in an open and forthright manner, the guide argues, the company can alleviate the anger and distress employees may feel at the prospect. Labor unions must cooperate if the program is to succeed; in most instances unions are pro-EAP but anti-drug testing. Companies must remember that their intent is to help the employee as well as the organization; if programs are designed with both concerns in mind, problems should be resolved to the benefit of all.

Legal issues take up the longest section of the guide. The issues: privacy, discrimination statutes, wrongful discharge actions and tort claims, defamation claims, arbitration issues, workers compensation, and federal statutes and safety regulations. The stress in this chapter is that individual companies must have legal counsel when they develop any type of substance abuse program, to protect both themselves and their employees.

The guide ends with examples of programs that are up and running. There are sample forms for testing and referrals, along with a list of testing methodologies that detail the advantages and short-comings of each. There is also a directory of information resources.

To raise employee awareness, NAWGA provides a 26-minute video entitled *Workplace Substance Abuse—An Intervention Model*. The video is not a dramatization like the Coronet/MTI films; instead, it consists of interviews with actual employees who have had substance abuse problems. They tell how drugs affected their performance both on and off the job.

Supporting this video are six brochures which describe various types, symptoms, and effects of drug abuse. Periodically distributed with worker paychecks, the brochures underline the company's commitment to the health, safety, and welfare of its employees.

Unique in its design for labor-based worksites, the NAWGA

83

program emphasizes employee safety and labor union relations. At $150 for the guide, video, and camera-ready boards for brochures, it is affordable and broad enough for use by any company involved in heavy industry.

CUSTOMIZED DRUG EDUCATION

A polished and comprehensive package directed toward a wider market is newly available from Random House, the New York based publishing house. AT $4,750—less, according to its marketers, than the cost of losing one employee to drug abuse—the "Stop Drugs at Work" program is worth a look.

"Stop Drugs at Work" is designed to communicate, educate, and raise the consciousness of both managers and employees. The package takes a turnkey approach by offering a variety of information along with a directory of consultants who may be of assistance to companies creating drug education programs.

The package includes five manuals, two videos, an "Update and Bulletin" service, and assorted visual paraphernalia. The titles of the printed material:

- Policy Formulation and Implementation Manual
- Facts About Drug Testing
- Guide for Supervisors
- Meeting Leaders Manual
- Facts About Drugs and Alcohol for Employers and Employees

These manuals take the reader through all the important issues that underlie the implementation of a drug education program. Together they provide managers, supervisors, and employees with information on the inherent dangers of drug abuse in the workplace.

The two video presentations are structured for different audiences. *The Policy Solution,* a drug education vehicle, aims at managers and supervisors; *Myths vs. Facts,* an awareness tool, is provided for employees. Both include interviews with the creators of the package: Dr. Mark S. Gold, founder of the National Cocaine Hotline; Peter Bensinger, former Administrator of the Drug Enforcement Administration; and Dr. Arnold M. Washton, Director of Addiction Research and Treatment at New York City's Regent Hospital. The employee video includes interviews with former drug addicts who discuss drug dependency and its effect upon work performance.

The Random House package provides continuing updates via a one-year subscription to the Update and Bulletin Service. Posters, buttons, and self-stick notes pads act as additional daily reminders of the dangers of drug abuse.

The Random House program is unique in its wealth of information resources, from the expertise that was combined in its fomulation to the directory of consultants who can provide additional information and support to individual company plans.

DRUG EDUCATION/DRUG AWARENESS

When favorite television programs are interrupted by floating faces prophesying the destructive power of drugs, and when sports heroes are more often seen denouncing drugs than selling cereal, the question occurs: are these spots doing any good? Does any sort of drug education truly treat the societal problem?

Lee Dogoloff, who heads the American Council for Drug Education, argues that the question misses the point. "Basically, when you are talking drug awareness, you not talking to the drug abuser. You are directing your message to the nonuser or the casual user.

"Fundamentally, only a minority—although a substantial minority—is using drugs," Dogoloff cautions. "And of this minority, only 10 to 15 percent are chemically dependent. This means that approximately 80 percent of those who use drugs choose to do so freely. If these people are made aware of the consequences of being detected as drug users—either being referred to treatment or being dismissed—in many cases they will stay off drugs."

Dogoloff emphasizes the dual tracks which companies must follow to be effective in combatting workplace substance abuse: drug *education* and drug *awareness*. Management cannot begin to tackle the problem of drug abuse if they don't know what it is, or what its effects are on both the employee and the company. Once *educated* to the dangers, management can begin the process of policy formulation, leading to further education of supervisors. The supervisor's job is to identify employees who may have a problem—to look for erratic behavior which may suggest a problem. But supervisors are not diagnosticians; it is for medical and human resources personnel to determine the presence of an individual drug problem. (The council can provide trainers who will assist an individual company's management in the education of drug abuse.)

Drug *awareness* proceeds apace. The American Council has designed a year-long campaign for companies to use: 12 payroll stuffers, each highlighting a particular aspect of drug abuse, and a set of three posters for worksite display. A managers' handbook provides additional support and ideas to use in conjunction with the material provided.

The strict distinction between education and awareness characterizes the American Council's approach. Education teaches management and supervisors the fundamentals of chemical dependence; awareness uses advertising vehicles which seek, through precise marketing, to change the perceptions of the audience, to reverse peer pressure, and to create general awareness. This program is not directed at the chemically dependent worker, but rather at the recreational user or the nonuser.

ONE TO ONE

Packages provide various materials; a consultant/trainer can walk a company through all the essentials of a drug abuse program. MGB Management Services, based in Olympia, Washington, is one of a growing number of private firms to enter this expanding field in recent years. As explained by MGB's Ron Kuest, its "Fitness For Work" program is a five-stage approach that can be adapted to specific company needs.

The first step is the development of company policy and procedure. Once this has been outlined, Mr. Kuest recommends that the CEO send a letter to every employee, stating the company's commitment to providing a safe and productive worksite. The letter anticipates frequently asked questions, and includes a question and answer sheet.

The next step concerns education of both supervisors and employees to the dangers of drug use. The supervisors receive training on how to spot and confront employees who appear to be impaired. The employee awareness training, an optional program, outlines the

THE STRAIGHT DOPE: Pamphlets from the American Council for Drug Education

new policy and discusses the impact of drug use on both the workplace and society in general. Also available are family awareness sessions. These are scheduled after work hours, and confront the issue of drug use in the family.

The "Fitness for Work" program does not look directly for drug abuse, but rather to an employee's actual fitness. According to Mr. Keust, "The concern is not so much with the legality or illegality of the substance, but with whether there is some sort of impairment causing that person to become unsafe or unproductive." A drug abuse problem in a worker's family may be a disruption to that employee's concentration—a point worth underscoring.

Also unique to this program is Mr. Keust's "re-entry contract." This contract states that once an employee is identified as having a drug or alcohol problem, he or she is put on probation until capable of returning to work. The employee must test negative for a particular substance and agree to continue the treatment process until a trained specialist certifies that treatment has been successful and that the employee's problem is no longer a concern to company safety. The re-entry contract may contain specific clauses pertaining to each individual's case—for example, suggesting that periodic testing take place. Usually, the re-entry contract lasts about twelve to eighteen months.

The key concept underlying the use of the materials is integration. None of these products is entirely freestanding. Some presuppose the existence of a working employee assistance program. Some imply that drug testing may be in use. But all are earnest attempts to give education and awareness its proper place in an overall corporate drug policy.

MORE TO COME

A great number of additional education and awareness materials will likely be available in the months ahead. The foregoing discussion presents a representative sample of materials available; it should not be taken as a recommendation or endorsement on the part of AMA.

4

EAPs: Addressing the Issues

EMPLOYEE ASSISTANCE PROGRAMS—or employee counseling programs (ECPs), the title in use in many federal agencies—grew out of pioneering attempts to deal with alcoholism among workers. In 1956 the American Medical Association defined alcoholism as a disease rather than a reflection of moral weakness; this rationale encouraged corporations to provide treatment and rehabilitation. By 1970, with the passage of the Hughes Act, federal funding became available; now the rationale was economic, as government, business, and labor leaders proclaimed the cost benefits of recognition and treatment.

The shift in emphasis to the economic impact of job impairment encouraged EAPs to focus on other emotional or personal problems which were affecting an individual's performance. Programs began to offer counseling for marital difficulties, debt management, depression, and finally drug dependency. While cost benefit remained a primary rationale there was, increasingly, a philosophical underpinning to such efforts—a philosophy reflected in corporate vocabulary, as "personnel practices" became "human resources management."

While AMA research confirms that an increasing number of companies are offering employee assistance and, through such programs, rehabilitative services to drug abusers, EAP professionals do not have the situation entirely in hand. "We don't have a handle on it, and I think we would be kidding ourselves if we said we did," warns Dr. Dale Masi. "The 'state of the art' in identifying drug abusers is in its infancy."

Dale Masi is Professor at the University of Maryland's School of Social Work and Community Planning, and adjunct professor at the university's College of Business and Management. She is also president of Masi Research Associates, and consults and evaluates the programs for IBM, Merrill Lynch, Bristol Myers, and the U.S. Department of Health and Human Services, among others. She has authored books on EAPs for AMACOM, publishing arm of the American Management Association, and served as a consultant for this AMA Research Report.

"Denial among drug users is even stronger than among alcoholics," says Dr. Masi. "Drug use has a greater variety of indicators, and yet there is a very narrow stereotype of the abuser. The tools that serve the EAP in the more familiar field of alcohol abuse are not necessarily useful in dealing with the abuse of illegal substances."

The problems mount with a confusion of roles. A troubled employee may be referred to an EAP for diagnosis and, if necessary, treatment. But if this diagnosis includes any sort of drug test, ought the EAP perform such a test?

Dr. Masi is definite in her opinion. "The EAP should not perform any testing, as this creates a conflict between the role of disciplinarian—which is not the EAP's job—and the concept of the EAP as a place where employees can voluntarily come for confidential help."

Dr. Masi is not alone in this concern. The Bureau of National Affairs' *Special Report on Alcohol and Drugs in the Workplace* states that "drug testing has emerged as a particularly troublesome issue for some EAPs." At root is "the fear...that employees will perceive a testing program as a detection and discipline device, and thereby destroy employees' trust that the employer is trying to help them—a critical element to EAP success." The BNA report goes on to quote Jim Mahoney, director of the assistance program run by the Philadelphia AFL-CIO, who cautions that a testing program "could kill your EAP."

The other side of the argument, from a western supplier of contracted EAP services: "Drug testing, if used judiciously and properly structured, may be compatible with EAPs." Certainly a drug test can be an important tool in breaking down the denial mechanisms upon which so many addicts depend. Confronted with medical proof, the drug abuser may be forced to face the problem. Tests may also monitor a patient's progress in treatment. William F. Alden, chief of the U.S. Drug Enforcement Administration's Congressional and Public Affairs Office, insists that "it is simply impossible to discuss drugs in the workplace without discussing testing." But the General Motors Corporation, with decades of experience in employee assistance, does not use drug testing in its program.

Dr. Masi is wary of using the EAP as a testing agent, and fears that some companies may use tests in place of assistance programs. "EAPs must develop a more aggressive stance to identify drug use," she says, so that companies will not resort to testing in the absence of other reliable methods of identification.

The more aggressive stance recommended by Dr. Masi requires additional training for EAP personnel. On intake, the EAP must go beyond the "presenting problem"—the problem that brought the employee to the EAP in the first place. "Counselors need to develop techniques to enable them to discern when the presenting problem is not the actual problem. They should look for drug abuse through more subtle signals, such as financial or marital difficulties, or a family history of alcohol. Screening tests should then be utilized."

EAPS: YOURS, MINE, AND OURS

Some organizations run thorough employee assistance programs entirely with in-hosue staff, but most companies lack the resources to support such a project in its entirety, or see benefit in using outside counseling firms. Alternatives are available: the consortium, in which a number of organizations band together to organize and maintain an EAP effort; and the contracted service. Where companies cannot or do not provide assistance, and employee union may offer help.

At IBM, an Employee Assistance Program began in July 1984. "We realized early on that to be used, our EAP had to guarantee total privacy," said Jim Parkel, IBM director of personnel programs, in a 1986 article in *Think*, the IBM magazine. "A major impediment to a person in a large company seeking help can be fear that even admitting the need for help might be a stigma. We felt the greatest assurance of confidentiality to employees, retirees and their families would be to use outside counseling firms."

According to Jim Daly, manager of employee assistance programs for IBM, outside counseling underlines the voluntary nature of the employee assistance program as well as its confidentiality. "There is no IBM intermediary between a person who needs help or advice and the EAP firm," Mr. Daly told a reporter for *Think*. Any IBM employee, retiree, or eligible family member can dial the EAP firm directly, at any hour of the day or night. At the counseling office, an employee waits in private waiting rooms, consults privately, and leaves via a private exit. IBM receives no record of client names, although it does get a regular count of those participating in the program.

Human Affairs International, Inc., is one of the two firms serving IBM; their client list also includes Exxon USA, Eastman Kodak, General Electric, USX, Coca-Cola and Monsanto. HAI president Otto Jones grants his own guarantee: "Our clients are entitled to have their privacy respected and ensured. Our credibility depends on it.

"After listening to the problem, we usually set up a schedule of appointments, which can run as few as one or as many as eight," Mr. Jones adds. "EAP is designed to provide short-term, goal-oriented counseling." For long-term treatment—the usual case in drug abuse problems—EAP counselors help clients choose from a list of prescreened private practitioners or community programs.

While HAI performs for IBM in the west and south, Personal Performance Consultants, Inc., covers the northeast and midwest. Lou Rosenfeld, senior consultant in charge of PPC's White Plains, N.Y., office, is prepared for anything in the way of personal problems requiring professional assistance. "We see literally everything here," Rosenfeld told *Think*. "People should know that all problems can be dealt with, whether through EAP or a referral."

Referral is an important element in the IBM program; HAI estimates that 20 percent of its IBM clients come because friends or coworkers recommend the program—a surprising figure, given the program's policy of confidentiality. A participant survey questionnaire, distributed by the counselor and mailed to IBM on a voluntary and anonymous basis, produced a 100 percent "yes" response to the question, "Was I treated in a confidential manner?"

The EAP supports IBM's testing-for-cause policies, but IBM

Notes for the Bottom Line

Three variables affect the annual cost of an employee assistance program:

- *population:* how many employees are served? May families and retirees call on EAP services?
- *location:* do most employees work at a single site, or are they widely scattered at multiple sites?
- *services:* is the EAP entirely a referral service with basically administrative duties, or does the EAP professional provide short-term counseling?

Recommended practice dictates one EAP professional (at an average of $35-40,000 per annum) for every 2,500 employees at a single site. Professional duties: responsibility for supervisory training and employee awareness and educational programs, as well as direct counseling and referrals to contracted services. In its first year, the EAP can expect a "Penetration rate" (number of employees seeking assistance) of 4 percent of the workforce.

Total cost? Dale Masi estimates a range, depending on the variables, of between $22 and $35 per worksite employee per year. Thus, for a worksite population of 2,500, the annual cost ranges from $55,000 to $87,500.

information representative Jim Burke emphasizes that participation in the EAP is strictly voluntary, not a matter of supervisory referral.

"Drug testing is not part of the EAP," Burke told AMA. "It's part of the 'for cause' testing function, but only in the sense that assistance is offered as an option to an employee who tests positive. We would recommend that he or she make use of the EAP, and in a sense you could call that a referral, but it is never mandatory.

"The EAP is part of IBM's overall wellness program, which includes the Plan for Life Personal Health Account and voluntary health screening. Employees are told of the availability of assistance, but essentially they use it on their own; it's strictly on a voluntary basis. Also, our medical benefits include payments for outpatient drug treatment.

"Managers at IBM have 40 hours of management training a year, and the majority of the training is on people management, Burke explained. "It would include how best to make use of such programs as EAPs and how to introduce them to employees."

"One of the real keys is the commitment we have from senior management," Burke reported. "Employees are urged to make full use of the program. Its availability is publicized in brochures and notices on bulletin boards. People are encouraged to make use of it."

CONSORTIA: MANY INTO ONE

A highly successful consortium has been operating in Taunton, Massachusetts since 1974, when it was first organized and incorporated as a nonprofit corporation. In that year, concerned members of the community met to discuss the problem of alcoholism among employees in the Taunton area.

The key players were the president of the Greater Taunton Council on Alcoholism; the administrator of the Substance Abuse Commission; and the Executive Director of the Taunton Chamber of Commerce. These three co-sponsored a seminar for forty leaders of fifteen area companies to assess alcoholism's impact in the workplace.

In that same year, Boston College's Occupational Alcohol and Drug Training program was searching for industrial sites to inaugurate treatment programs. The Taunton Chamber of Commerce invited Dr. Dale Masi, then at Boston College, to discuss EAPs with business leaders; the result was an agreement among ten Taunton companies to form a consortium, to be staffed and guided by the college.

A consortium committee was formed, consisting of representatives from the ten companies; Boston College's community organization intern; and members of the Taunton Chamber of Commerce, with the particular support of its executive director. The committee's tasks:

- A needs assessment for the community as a whole and for the individual participating companies.
- Policy formulation for the consortium and for each company.

- A training program for supervisors who would identify and refer employees with work performance problems.
- Development of an information and referral network.
- Dissemination of information on alcoholism. This program later expanded to include other personal problems, including drug addiction.

Each committee participant served as the liaison between the home company and the consortium, and was responsible for implementation of the program at the company. As a group, the committee would evaluate the program on an ongoing basis.

The community organizer was assigned the actual implementation of the consortium program, and served as coordinator. She assisted each company with policy development and supervisory training and education. She also contacted treatment agencies and organized a system for employee referral.

In 1975, a caseworker joined the staff and took responsibility for diagnosing employees and referring them to local community agencies. The caseworker provided ongoing counseling when appropriate.

By the end of the first year, the consortium had been incorporated as a nonprofit organization, thus limiting its liability and giving it the power to enter into contracts. The original consortium committee became the board of directors and drew up bylaws.

In 1978, six companies from nearby Brockton joined the consortium, and its name was changed from the Taunton Area EAP to EAP, Inc. Its offices are maintained at a hospital in Taunton and at a local social service agency in Brockton.

Today, more than 25 companies participate. According to Charles Volkman, who was the Taunton Chamber of Commerce Executive Director in 1974 and is today its Treasurer, EAP, Inc.'s current staff includes a full-time director and one full-time and two part-time social workers. It has two contracts with the State of Massachusetts to provide intake and referral services, and serves the City of Taunton, including the police and fire departments, teachers in the school system, and City Hall employees.

"We really did it on a shoestring," Mr. Volkman recalls of the consortium's early days. "We had to show the business community that it would work." A good working knowledge of the business community is vital to any consortium, he emphasizes.

EAP ON CALL: THE CONTRACTED SERVICE

A full-blown EAP features preventive services—drug awareness and education programs and counseling—as well as treatment and/or referral. An increasing number of companies provide such rounded activities to organizations which prefer outside provision of such service.

An example: Plan 21, a Houston-area business which offers "mental wellness" programs to corporations. A Plan 21 spokesperson listed these benefits to the employer:

- Cost containment with effective early problem intervention.
- Lower overall insurance rate increases, as indicated in a recent study of 221 corporations by the International Foundation of Employee Benefit Plans. Rate increases were higher for companies which did not include EAPs in their benefits packages.
- Fewer claims for psychological and physical disorders.
- Increased employee performance and mental wellness, resulting in reduced absenteeism, less use of sick days, higher productivity, and higher overall morale.

Plan 21 features a 24-hour answering service for troubled employees. Its counselors provide help on a short-term basis. For long-term help, Plan 21 makes referrals to suitable facilities.

Costs are key. "Because of meagre outpatient but available inpatient psychiatric coverage, the resulting tendency proves to be an increase in expensive hospitalization for treatment," the spokesperson points out. By providing a package that combines affordable outpatient treatment with a tailor-made benefits package, Plan 21 offers what it terms a "true wellness solution"—that is, prevention, as opposed to treatment offered only when an employee's condition warrants hospitalization—or when an employee cannot obtain insured treatment outside of a hospital.

UNION EAPS: TAKING CARE OF OUR OWN

The course of labor-management relations has seldom run smooth. The authors of the BNA Special Report sum it up: "Workers' desire for autonomy in their personal lives has repeatedly conflicted with employers' needs for discipline in the workplace. . .The newer, less familiar issue of drug use has further complicated this delicate area of employment relations. Mishandled, the question of substance abuse has the potential for disrupting, even poisoning relations between employers and employees."

Union members often regard company-run EAPs as management tools, ways of winning employees to managment's side. Where the union is regarded as an employee advocate, with people as its main concern, management is seen as viewing profits as their sole end. Management may be concerned with the impact of drug abuse on the bottom line, the union holds, but does it really care about the human side of drug abuse?

The Association of Flight Attendants, AFL-CIO, established a union-based employee assistance program in 1978. The Washington Business Group on Health, in its Worksite Wellness Media Report, summed up the unique conditions and special needs that gathered around 21,000-member union:

> Most employee assistance programs rely on supervisors to recognize signs of impaired job performance and to refer employees for counseling and assistance. Flight attendants are a highly mobile workforce, with irregular hours, who do their work with a minimum of supervision. Clearly a different approach was needed and the result was a peer model EAP that relies heavily on concerned volunteers who possess the qualities necessary to be effective in helping troubled employees. After receiving training, local EAP committees select and evaluate service providers and treatment facilities, circulate information about the existence of the EAP and how to gain access to its help, identify and intervene with troubled employees, keep case records, and provide data to union headquarters.

Barbara Feuer, director of the flight attendants' EAP, expanded on the program's peer referral aspect when interviewed by AMA researchers. The key: training flight attendants to be "health ambassadors."

"The 'health ambassadors' were the EAP Committee members," Ms. Feuer explained, recalling the program's initiation in 1978. "We identified people in the workplace who were well liked, who were accessible, who could be trusted, who could abide by confidentiality, and who were motivated to help their co-workers. They were people who were with the flight attendants all the time.

"We don't train them to be diagnosticians; we train them to recognize problem behavior and to be able to refer people to appropriate treatment resources or self-help groups. And the training that we offer in Washington is really state-of-the-art. They learn how to intervene formally and informally; they learn about the diseases of alcoholism and drug addiction, about women and alcoholism. We have a predominantly female work population. They learn about crisis intervention, suicide prevention, and about working with victims of rape. They learn about domestic violence and eating disorders. They learn about all of these human problems.

"The key element is the crisis intervention concept. Trainees do a lot of role playing, a lot of experimental techniques. The training is four days of very intensive work, and when they get back to work they get a lot of ongoing training."

The flight attendants' workspace is also unique—"a giant tube," Ms. Feuer calls it—and the constant travel with an ever-changing cast of peers is an additional special feature. "A pattern emerges," Ms. Feuer said. "You have no idea what's behind it—or maybe you do, maybe you have some kind of inkling, maybe you see her do something. In such an instance, a co-worker doesn't really know how to handle it. She doesn't know how to intervene. But what a flight attendant can do is contact a committee member, or call the national office by an 800 number. Then we can work with the caller on how to approach the co-worker concerned."

After identification, rehabilitation. "EAP committee members are responsible for developing community treatment resources within their own communities—psychologists who can do a differential diagnosis to screen out alcohol or other drug abuse, psychiatrists, social workers, safehouses for battered women, financial assistance, whatever," Ms. Feuer reported. "They and their committees develop the resources. We give them a lot of screening information, questions to ask, forms to use to make sure they're getting the best resources possible. We believe that the committee members are in a position to identify the resources that are going to best serve their population—a population where someone might not be able to make their meeting or appointment every week, or during aftercare can't come in every single week. The committee members have the skills to find resources that are going to be receptive to that type of lifestyle and the kind of special needs that the flight attendant might have.

"If the person needs to be referred and admits they've got a problem, the committee members know what the insurance policy is for their particular airline and can then make the referral, because they've got the cadre of resources."

In place of a disciplinary warning from management, the union members send a different message. "Our leverage is to say, 'We are your advocates, we are your union, but you can only continue this kind of behavior for so long before the company's going to get involved, and then you're going to be subject to some kind of discipline and be in more trouble,'" Ms. Feuer said. "'Then it will be harder for us to help you.'"

But management has become less a source of potential discipline than a partner in the endeavor, Ms. Feuer reported. "When we first got this grant, one of the goals was to develop a joint program with the company," she recalled. "However, since it was a time of deregulation of the airline industry and a lot of companies were scrambling to survive, they never really picked up on it. They saw that our people were really helping, and they began to refer to us. Seventeen percent of our referrals in 1986 were from supervisors or other management personnel.

"The traditional adversarial relationship fell by the wayside here. Our committee members will say to management, 'We can help you, and we need you to help us, to refer people in trouble instead of disciplining them.' They say, 'We're all overworked and underpaid. We don't know how to identify this kind of problem. We don't have the expertise. Yes, we'll work with you on it.' Every year, the percentage of referrals from management has gone up.

"There's a direct benefit," Ms. Feuer summarized. "We can work with people with addiction problems before they get involved in the disciplinary process. It makes everybody's job a little easier. Our attorneys say there's no question but that there are fewer grievances on drug and alcohol cases as a result of this program."

REHABILITATION: THE COST ISSUE

At present, the insurance coverage offered by most U.S. companies does not extend to outpatient drug addiction treatment. On the other hand, these policies do cover hospitalization costs for detoxification and inpatient treatment—often quite generously. What exactly are these costs?

A recent *Washington Post* article* pointed out that the most publicized alcohol and drug abuse centers, the Fair Oaks Hospital Group (home of the famous 800-COCAINE hotline), carries a thousand-dollar-a-day price tag—higher than the price of a day in the coronary care unit of Massachusetts General Hospital. The full inpatient treatment, ranging from four weeks to six months, is billed at an average of $56,000, with a high of $160,000 and a low of $28,000.

"This is a spread whose lower end is higher than the cost of bypass surgery and all its attendant expenses," the *Post* noted, "and whose upper end is more than double the average cost—$70,000—of treating an AIDS patient. Most other middle-class centers cost $10,000 per term of treatment, while the Betty Ford Center charges $5,000, and Hazelton in Minnesota charges $4,000."

The *Post* also cites a U.S. Alcohol, Drug Abuse and Mental Health Administration figure on the current annual cost of insurance: $6 billion annually to treat less than 5 percent of addicts and alcoholics. "Extrapolate from this to the entire population of addicts and alcoholics needing help and the cost comes to $120 billion a year—for one term of treatment," the *Post* went on.

Clearly, there has to be another way. A solution suggested by a number of the experts we interviewed, calls for more outpatient treatment—and added insurance coverage for this treatment. Dr. Richard Rawson, Executive Director of the Matrix Center in Beverly Hills, an outpatient addiction center, points to figures from a study he is currently conducting:

> "In this first study the cost of the hospitalization was approximately $12,000 per 28-day episode. If a psychiatrist follows the patient in the hospital, an additional $3,500 charge was incurred. The cost of the outpatient episode was $3,600 for six months."

West Coast treatment costs are considerably lower than those in the East.

More coverage for outpatient therapy is one workable solution to the cost differential. IBM has recently announced new benefits that expand coverage for outpatient drug and alcohol treatment. "Our hope is that by providing benefits that are more flexible and with

*"The Drug Users: Can They Affort Treatment?", Toby Cohen, August 8, 1986.

greater options, this will enable people who need help to obtain the kind of care that is required," states Bill Ehrich, IBM's Corporate Manager of Health and Medical Benefits.

Some illegal drugs are physically addictive; others are not. "Casual" users may require simple counseling; those with a true addiction require detoxification and ongoing rehabilitative treatment. Some programs offer direct treatment by medical staffers; others refer drug abusers to hospitals or outpatient clinics with established detoxification and rehabilitation services. Experts differ on methodology, and therefore EAP personnel ought to be knowledgable about various treatment techniques.

There is preliminary and fragmentary statistical evidence that outpatient treatment that includes drug therapy can be successful. A study* of drug users recruited from a cocaine "hotline" and treatment program divided 83 subjects into three self-selected groups: those receiving no formal treatment; those hospitalized for an average of three weeks and then referred to voluntary aftercare; and those in continuing outpatient care employing drug therapy for six months. The percentages returning to monthly cocaine use in the eight months following the initial interview:

No formal treatment:	47 percent
Inpatient hospitalization:	43 percent
Outpatient care/plus medication:	13 percent

"Current hospital aftercare programs may not be appropriately oriented for cocaine users," the authors of the study concluded. "It appears the hospital program in this study retained fewer than 30 percent of the subjects in aftercare." Considering the costs involved in inpatient drug abuse treatment, the poor success rate documented in this study is staggering.

"Outpatient treatment for cocaine dependency is a viable form of treatment in which subjects will participate for up to six months on a fee-for-service basis," the study concluded, with the caveat that "this conclusion is extremely guarded due to a large number of methodological issues and the short follow-up period."

*Cocaine Treatment Outcome: Cocaine Use Following Inpatient, Outpatient, and No Treatment, Richard A. Rawson et. al., in Proceedings, 1985 Meeting, Committee on Problems of Drug Dependence, Inc.

Dr. David Ockert of New York City's Parallax Center has been tracking data on the success of his outpatient program, which employs drug therapy, and finds the same percentage of patients remaining drug-free: 87 percent. He lists other advantages to such treatment.

"An outpatient treatment for drug abuse is not only less expensive than hospitalization," Dr. Ockert explains, "it allows the individual to remain in the community, at home, and in the workplace, so the cost, both emotional and financial, is less for both the individual and the employer than in-patient hospitalization would be."

The very thing that makes a hospital effective for detoxification—its restrictive environment—may foreshadow a relapse for the released patient, Dr. Ockert explains. "In a hospital you don't have your normal environmental triggers, and you know you can't get the drug. There are studies that show that the number of impulses for, say, alcohol is significantly lower while someone is an inpatient. So an outpatient facility has a number of benefits to the patient, as well as to the insurance company and the employer, since it's much less expensive.

"Of course, some people have to go to the hospital for detox. Sometimes the withdrawal can be severe, even with medication. But it's much more effective to keep someone in a community with their families so that they can be productive and remain in the workplace. In this way they learn adaptive reactions—how to react differently to environmental stresses. Taking drugs is a nonadaptive reaction. Drug abusers have to learn to live without getting high.

"Hospitals are very good at detox. Where they fall down is aftercare. Somebody gets very intensive treatment in a hospital facility, but when they get out there is no adequate access to intensive professional help and support. Outpatient addiction treatment facilities offer both talk therapy and medication adjuncts."

Dr. Ockert describes the Parallax Center's brand of outpatient treatment: "It's very intensive. Three days a week, three individual sessions a week and one group a week. This can go on for quite some time, usually six months to a year. It offers intensive treatment to work through a lot of the problems and issues so that the person learns to react differently to life events, where in the past they would turn to drugs. They learn to stay away from people, places, and things that trigger their impulses."

In defense of the program's most controversial feature—antidepressant medication used to stabilize the patient's post-detox mood swings—Dr. Ockert looks to the wider context of drug addiction.

"Let me explain about withdrawal from drugs," he says. "Cocaine, like heroin, is extremely physically addictive. With both, staying off the drug [after detoxification] is the difficult problem. After 20 or 30 days off the drug there is a constellation of symptoms—the protracted abstinance syndrome—because the person is biochemically out of balance. This can be detected physiologically—measurements you can take to determine that someone has been affected by the drug even though it is completely out of the system.

"The concept is calleld neuroadaptation. Basically, the body becomes chemically adapted to the drug. The body chemistry is altered so much that it takes about six months to a year in order to find the homeostasis, or equilibrium, that is normal. And during that time the individual is subject to incredible mood swings. Their moods can swing from a high-energy agitation to a low-energy depression, and they are not armed with the biochemistry of a non-addict to deal with the problems that come up.

"People just out of detox are so emotionally uncomfortable, suffering from depression and periods of agitation," Dr. Ockert emphasizes. "The only way they know how to handle this is to get high. Which is why I use mood stabilizing medication such as antidepressants. They are not addictive or euphoric. There is no withdrawal, and it's a short-term, low dose protocol.

"The neuroadaptation I have described is probably true of heroin, alcohol, and cocaine, although different hormones are probably involved with different drugs. But since cocaine does not have the physical withdrawal discomfort of alcohol and heroin, many people in the past would not classify it as an addictive drug. Now, with the concept of neuroadaptation—the fact that the person is disoriented biochemically for a long time—cocaine addiction fits right in."

Dr. Ockert works through corporate EAPs to train supervisors to detect signs and symptoms of drug abuse among their workers, but does so "on a very selective basis, when I know the company is interested in helping the addict." The keys to watch: repeatedly late or constantly reporting in sick, with lower work productivity.

"It's not so easy to be sure," Dr. Ockert warns. "The problem with looking for signs and symptoms is that someone who is snorting a great deal of cocaine may be constantly sniffling and have teary eyes, and be late for work, and irritable and uncomfortable—or he could have the flu. You have to see these signs and symptoms repeatedly over time, and a deteriorating work performance over time. Absenteeism, lateness, leaving early, long lunch hours. I don't expect the manager to get into the personal life of the employee, but maybe at that time he or she could refer the worker to the EAP, if the company has one, or to its medical services.

"The supervisor usually refers them to an EAP on the basis of performance," Dr. Ockert emphasizes, "and the EAP then refers patients to me because my treatment enables people to stay on the job. Really, the bottom line is the success rate, the outcome six months or a year after treatment—whether the person is using drugs or not. The outcome can be measured. It's not unclear, like it is with psychotherapy, where it's hard to pinpoint when someone is better. In drug abuse it is certainly much clearer."

Appendix I
Survey Statistics

This appendix contains additional statistics from our 1,090 survey respondents.

A.1. Respondents testing or not testing for drug use, by industry.

Industry	Number of Respondents	Testing (Percent)	Not testing (Percent)
Diversified conglomerate	24	29	71
Banking/finance	69	3	97
Communications/publishing	33	9	91
Education	42	0	100
Electronics	46	20	80
Entertainment/lodging	19	10	90
Food processing/agribusiness	33	33	66
Government	77	22	78
Healthcare	112	15	85
Insurance	34	6	94
Manufacturing: consumer goods	109	22	78
Manufacturing: industrial goods	165	40	60
Mineral extraction	14	71	29
Professional services	46	9	91
Trade (wholesale/retail)	41	20	80
Transportation/distribution	32	56	56
Utilities	26	26	38
All others	168	14	86
Total	1090	21	79

A.2. If the company is not testing for substance abuse, what action has it taken on the testing issue?

Industry	Number	Percent			
		Now developing drug testing program	Rejected testing	Using techniques other than testing	No position taken
Diversified conglomerate	17	31	7	12	41
Banking/finance	67	4	7	6	79
Communications/ publishing	30	10	10	13	63
Education	42	0	7	12	81
Electronics	37	16	22	16	46
Entertainment/ lodging	17	6	6	6	65
Food processing/ agribusiness	22	36	9	0	45
Government	60	22	7	13	52
Healthcare	94	18	13	15	55
Insurance	32	3	13	3	84
Manufacturing: consumer	85	21	15	7	54
Manufacturing: industrial	99	20	6	12	59
Mineral extraction	4	0	0	0	75
Professional services	42	0	14	14	76
Trade	33	21	15	9	52
Utilities	16	31	13	19	25
All others	118	8	11	8	67

A.3. If the company is not testing for abuse, is there a written policy on substance abuse in place?

Yes, a policy is in place	25 percent
A policy is now being written	24
No policy/no plans to develop one	46

A.4. Regional perspective—companies testing or not testing.

Zip Code (first digit)	States	Number	Percent testing	Percent not testing
0	Maine, New Hampshire, Vermont, Massachusetts, Rhode Island, Connecticut	150	28	72
1	New York, New Jersey, Pennsylvania	117	17	83
2	Maryland, Delaware, District of Columbia, Virginia, North Carolina, South Carolina	76	17	83
3	Tennessee, Georgia, Florida, Alabama	67	23	77
4	Ohio, Indiana, Michigan, Kentucky	128	25	75
5	Wisconsin, Minnesota, Iowa, North Dakota, South Dakota, Montana	94	14	86
6	Illinois, Missouri, Nebraska, Kansas	108	21	79
7	Louisiana, Arkansas, Oklahoma, Texas	79	25	75
8	New Mexico, Arizona, Colorado, Utah, Wyoming, Idaho, Nevada	52	08	92
9	California, Oregon, Washington, Alaska, Hawaii	179	24	76

A.5. Companies testing/not testing by company size

Number of employees, all company locations	Total Respondents	Percent testing	Percent not testing
Fewer than 500	470	16	84
500 to 2,499	338	23	77
2,500 to 4,999	90	21	79
5,000 or more	151	36	63

Annual Sales or Budget	Total respondents	Percent testing	Percent not testing
Under $50	448	15	85
$50 Million to 199 Million	245	23	77
$200 Million to 499 Million	121	25	75
$500 Million to $1 billion	79	28	72
$1 billion or more	97	39	61
No answer	88	9	91

The questionnaire used two questions to gauge company size: number of employees, all locations, and annual sales (annual budget if nonprofit).

The larger the company, the more likely it is to have a drug testing program. Many of our respondents, however, come from small companies, with 15 to 16 percent of these engaged in testing programs.

Exhibit A.6. Companies testing: respondent base by company size.

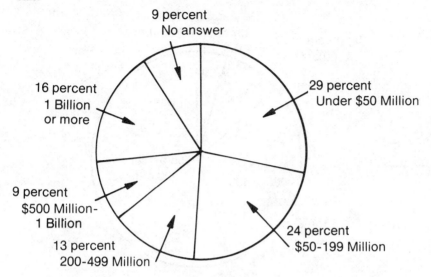

9 percent
No answer

29 percent
Under $50 Million

16 percent
1 Billion
or more

24 percent
$50-199 Million

9 percent
$500 Million-
1 Billion

13 percent
200-499 Million

Annual sales or budget

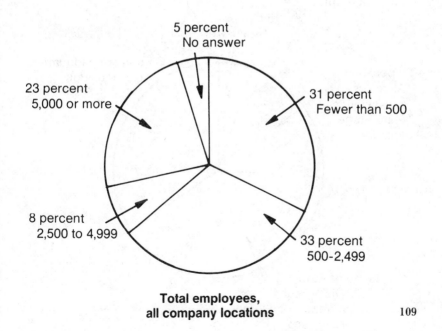

5 percent
No answer

23 percent
5,000 or more

31 percent
Fewer than 500

8 percent
2,500 to 4,999

33 percent
500-2,499

**Total employees,
all company locations**

Exhibit A.7. Companies testing: respondent base by worksite population.

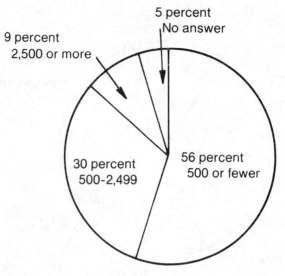

5 percent
No answer

9 percent
2,500 or more

30 percent
500-2,499

56 percent
500 or fewer

Exhibit A.8. Companies testing: respondent base by organizational description.

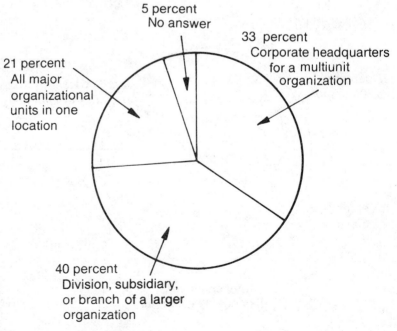

5 percent
No answer

21 percent
All major
organizational
units in one
location

33 percent
Corporate headquarters
for a multiunit
organization

40 percent
Division, subsidiary,
or branch of a larger
organization

Appendix II
Questions and Answers about Drug Testing Technology

Victoria Bannister
Abbott Laboratories

This appendix contains answers to questions that are frequently asked of Abbott Laboratories representatives.

What are the components of a workplace drug testing program?

Before any testing is begun, the company should carefully evaluate the reasons for testing for drugs. Then, working with legal counsel, the company should draft a policy that defines the reasons for testing and the consequences for those employees who are identified by the process. The policy should be communicated to all employees well in advance of implementation.

In defining the testing process itself, the company should choose screening and confirmation methods appropriate for its needs. It should choose between on-site or off-site screening methods; establish chain of custody procedures for sample handling; write a standard operating procedure for the sample collection, testing, and results-reporting process; and, finally, establish a quality assurance program for the total process.

Can drug testing show level of impairment?

Positive results of a urine screen cannot be used to prove intoxication or level of impairment. Drugs and drug metabolites may appear in the urine for several days or weeks after the drug was last used. Urine drug screens only provide evidence of prior drug use.

What is a "urine screen" and what is a confirmation test?

A screen is a test or series of tests that distinguish negative samples from those that may contain the drug in question.

If a druglike compound is found, the laboratory may perform a confirmatory test to ensure that the druglike compound was an abused drug rather than an artifact such as an over-the-counter medication.

A confirmation is a test using an alternate method that is specific and at least as sensitive as the original screen.

What are the primary methods for screening?

Screening methods generally fall into two categories: immuno-assays and thin layer chromatography (TLC).

Immunoassays are based on the principle of competition between labeled and unlabeled antigen (drug) for binding sites on an antibody which has been developed for the drug class in question. Antibodies are protein substances with sites on their surface to which specific drugs or drug metabolites will bind. In general terms, immunoassays differ by the type of label used, the instrumentation designed to measure the amount of binding, and the quality of the initial chemistry used to prepare the antibody. The radioimmunoassay (RIA) uses a radioactive label; the enzyme immunoassay (EIA) uses an enzyme label; and the fluorescence polarization immunoassay (FPIA) uses a fluorescent label.

In thin layer chromatography an absorbent material is applied to a plate. Extractions of drugs from the urine are applied to the plates which are then exposed to different chemicals. The drugs separate and migrate up the plate; the drugs are identified through visual recognition of the position and color of the spot on the plate.

Who manufactures the various screening methods?

Three major immunoassay manufacturers are:

1. FPIA -
Abbott Diagnostics Division

Abbott Laboratories
Abbott Park, IL 60064
800-323-9100

2. RIA
Roche Diagnostics, Inc.
Nutley, NJ 07110
201-235-6500

3. EIA
Syva Company
Palo Alto, CA 94304
415-493-2200

The major commercial system with standardized TLC is man-ufactured by Analytical Systems, Laguna Hills, CA.

What are the different confirmation methods?

Under appropriate conditions confirmation tests can include immunoassays, TLC, HPLC, GC (GLC) and GC/MS. The HPLC GC and GC/MS are sophisticated instrumental methods requiring highly trained technicians to operate them.

What is the preferred method for confirmation?

The gold standard for court cases is gas chromatography coupled with mass spectrometry (GC/MS).

How accurate and reliable are the various screening methods?

Accuracy and reliability must be assessed in the context of the total laboratory system. Each manufacturer's or laboratory's claims for precision, specificity, and sensitivity should be evaluated. Also important to accuracy and reliability are the training of the personnel and the adherence to quality control procedures, to the man-ufacturer's protocols, and to chain of custody for the whole process.

What are precision, sensitivity, specificity, and Threshold?

Precision is the ability to get the same results between repeated measurements. The measurement term for this is coefficient of variation, or "CV". The lower the CV, the more precise is the method. Lack of precision can lead to false positives and false negatives.

Sensitivity is the lowest concentration of a drug that can be reliably detected by a particular test procedure. Lack of sensitivity can lead to false negatives.

Specificity is the ability to identify a single drug or class of chemical components in a mixture of chemicals or biological materials. Lack of specificity can lead to false positives.

Threshold, or cutoff, is the defined value that determines the presence or absence of a drug or drug metabolites. Samples containing drugs at concentration levels greater than or equal to Threshold are reported as "Above the Threshold" or "Positive"; samples with concentrations below the chosen Threshold are reported as "Less Than Threshold" and are generally reported as negative, though in fact, the sample could contain the drug in question.

Establishing Thresholds that are very high increases the number of false negatives. Setting the Threshold as low as possible allows for longer detection time after drug administration but can cause difficulties in confirmation.

How long can drugs be detected?

Detection times vary from drug to drug and from person to person, and depend on the sensitivity of the drug chosen. The more sensitive the test method, the longer the drug can be detected. Individual differences in metabolism can affect the detection time. Some drugs can be detected for much longer times than others; for example, cocaine can be detected for two to four days; marijuana can be detected up to several weeks for chronic smokers.

What drugs are commonly abused?

Alcohol is the most commonly used drug with approximately 100 million users in the United States. Marijuana and cocaine follow

114

with an estimated 20 million and 5 million users, respectively. Other less commonly abused drugs in the United States include amphetamines, benzodiazepines (Librium™, Valium™), barbiturates, opiates, and PCP.

What are the advantages to testing on-site?

Advantages include;

1. Simplified chain of custody and sample control
2. Greater sense of confidentiality
3. Immediate results
4. Reduced costs
5. Reduced paperwork

What are the advantages to choosing an outside laboratory?

The advantages center on the professional capabilities of the laboratory that may not be available at the on-site testing facility. These include:

1. Fully trained staff
2. Ready availability of confirmatory methods
3. Availability of staff to serve as expert witnesses
4. Established specimen storage and collection procedures

Utilizing an outside laboratory does not relieve the company of its overall legal responsibility for proper handling of samples.

What factors should be considered in choosing a lab?

- Find out if the lab is licensed in any government programs and how well the lab has performed in any proficiency programs.
- Review the laboratory's standard operating procedures.
- Inspect the physical plant and observe the organization and procedures.
- Review and inspect the chain of custody procedures.
- Determine with the laboratory a procedure for handling flawed samples.

- Insure that samples are appropriately identified throughout the process and that sample integrity is maintained.
- Review the staff's professional credentials.
- Review and inspect evidence of the laboratory's ongoing quality control and quality assurance program. This should include participation in a proficiency program. The laboratory should also be prepared to receive blind proficiency samples from the client.
- Consider the laboratory's business reputation.
- Price should be the last consideration in the selection of a laboratory. The cost to the company of one improperly handled laboratory test could be far greater than any savings in laboratory testing fees.
- Determine if all results are reviewed by a senior certifying official before they are reported to the client. Define whether that certifying official or other personnel will be available to defend results in the event of legal or labor actions.
- Identify what supplies or services are included in price such as specimen containers, chain of custody forms, adherence to chain of custody procedures, or courier services.
- Contract for a specific turnaround time and insure that both parties have full understanding of times for screening and confirmation.
- Examine equipment used for testing; determine if equipment is used in accordance with manufacturer's recommendations.
- Obtain agreement for the right to make periodic inspections by either the contracting organization or an outside expert in the area of laboratory audits.

Appendix III
Sample Company Policies

This appendix contains two examples of company policies. For the first of these, the respondent has asked that the company name be removed. The corporate medical director will, however, answer serious inquiries about the policy and how it was formulated. See note at the end of the policy.

The second policy comes from Philips Industries, Inc.

Both policies are presented for purposes of illustration only.

HUMAN RESOURCE GUIDES
ALCOHOL AND DRUGS

A. USE OF ALCOHOL

No employee may report to work or work while under the influence of alcohol.[1] The use, sale, purchase, transfer or possession of alcohol in any company facility (including parking lots) or company provided vehicle is prohibited. However, the consumption of alcohol in the passenger section of an airplane or its storage in a sealed container in the trunk or other compartment of an employee's personal vehicle parked on a company lot is not prohibited.

Any employee may not normally consume alcohol anywhere during rest breaks, lunches or other meals if the employee must work thereafter on the same day. However, it may be permissible to consume alcohol in moderation at business lunches not exclusively attended by the Company's employees or at conferences or conventions. Such consumption of alcohol is not encouraged by the Company and must be limited so that it does not affect the employee's

---

[1]"Under the influence" means, for the purpose of this policy, that the employee is affected by alcohol or other drugs or the combination in any detectable manner. The presence of influence is not confined to obvious impairment of physical or mental ability, such as slurred speech or diffculty in maintaining balance but may be established by a professional opinion, a scientifically valid test, and in some cases such as alcohol, by a lay person's observation.

safety, the safety of co-workers, members of the public or the employee's job performance.

B. USE OF LEGAL DRUGS

A "legal drug" is a prescribed drug or over-the-counter drug which has been legally obtained and is being used for the purposes for which it was prescribed or manufactured.

Being under the influence of any legally obtained drug by any employee while performing company business or while in a company facility (including a parking lot) or in any company provided vehicle is prohibited to the extent that such use or influence may affect the employee's safety, the safety of co-workers or members of the public or the employee's job performance. If, in the judgment of a company doctor or nurse or other health care professional, such is the case, the employee will either (1) be placed in a restricted job, (2) given altered responsibilities, (3) with the concurrence of the prescribing physician placed on an alternate drug or dosage.

C. USE OF ILLEGAL DRUGS

An "illegal drug" is any drug which cannot be legally obtained (e.g., marijuana, narcotics, hallucinogens, etc.), or which although legal has been illegally obtained, (e.g. prescribed drugs not legally obtained or prescribed drugs not being used for prescribed purposes).

The use, sale, purchase, transfer or possession in any amount of an illegal drug by any employee at any time during working hours (including meal breaks or rest breaks), at any time while on company business, at any time while in a company facility including parking lots, or in any company provided vehicle is prohibited.

D. DRUG AND ALCOHOL TESTING, ASSESSMENT AND REHABILITATION

Business units may, with the approval of the cognizant Executive Vice President and the Vice President of Human Resources, implement a procedure for health assessments which may include drug and alcohol testing in compliance with the following guidelines:

(a) *Current Employees*
    Business units may request that an employee submit to a

118

health assessment which may include a blood test, urinalysis or other drug/alcohol test where the employee's behavior, performance and/or safety/accident record indicate that a health problem may exist including the probability of drug and/or alcohol use prohibited above. If the employee refuses, such refusal may together with other factors be considered in determining appropriate job assignment or disciplinary action.

Where safety, security or customers' requirements relating to a job or category of jobs justifies testing, business units may request a blood test, urinalysis or other drug/alcohol testing of employees' assigned, or to be assigned, to such a job or as a condition of remaining on or being assigned to the job.

Employees reporting to work or working who are suspected of being under the influence of alcohol or other drugs should be taken to a health care provider for a health assessment which may include alcohol/drug testing and/or a referral for a chemical dependency assessment.

Employees shall be given an opportunity to inform the health professional and/or the laboratory performing the testing of any prescription/or over-the-counter medications they may be taking at the time of testing.

Where employees are represented by a union, the union should be advised of an intent to request such tests before they are made and be permitted to negotiate on the matter if the union so desires. (This does not apply to testing of applicants.)

Business units located in the same metropolitan area should coordinate drug testing policies and procedures.

All employee drug screening tests that are positive should be followed by a confirmation test using the same blood or urine sample used in the screening test. It will be the responsibility of the health care professional and/or the laboratory performing the test(s) to insure that the "chain of custody" safeguards have been met with regard to the collection, storage, transportation and delivery of the specimens of employees that undergo testing. If the confirmation test is positive, the employee should be referred to an EAP program for an assessment for chemical dependency. The employee should be required to follow an appropriate plan of corrective action which may include follow-up drug testing. If the employee refuses to accept the referral to an EAP program for a chemical dependency assessment and/or follow an appropriate plan of corrective action, take appropriate disciplinary action.

If the employee presents an actual safety or security risk, he should not be allowed to continue his job until the risk has abated. This may involve suspending the employee, placing him on leave or, where rehabilitation efforts have failed, termination.

No testing should be conducted without the employee's concurrence. Request should be made in a manner calculated to preserve the employee's privacy and dignity. Thus, knowledge of the request and the result should be limited to those who have a need to know. Under no circumstances should it be made a matter of general information unless the employee chooses to make such communications.

Where sale or possession of illegal drugs on company premises is suspected, normal surveillance and investigative techniques including referral to law enforcement authorities should be used.

(b) *Testing Applicants*

Business units may at their option initiate policies and procedures for drug testing of:

- All applicants considered for employment;
- Applicants selected on a random basis;
- Applicants for particular jobs or areas of work;
- Applicants extended offers contingent on "negative results" of the test; or
- None of its applicants.

Where a policy of testing for drugs is adopted, applicants should be clearly notified and advised that they will not be considered or retained, should they be conditionally hired, unless a negative test is obtained. Applicants refusing to take a test should not be further considered for employment.

120

NOTE: Maine, Minnesota and Massachusetts bar the use of a medical examination or the obtaining of medical information from an applicant until after an offer of employment has been made, contingent of a finding that the person meets the physical and mental requirements of the job. Therefore in these states no drug testing should be done until applicants are extended job offers contingent upon "negative results" of drug testing.

All applicant drug screening tests that are positive should be followed by a confirmation test using the same blood and/or urine sample used in the screening test. It will be the responsibility of the health care professional and/or the laboratory performing the test(s) to insure that the "chain of custody" safeguards have been met with regard to the collection, storage, transportation and delivery of the specimens of applicants who undergo testing.

Applicants shall be given an opportunity to inform the health professional and/or laboratory performing the testing of any prescription and/or over-the-counter medications they may be taking at the time of testing.

If the confirmation test is positive the applicant should be advised, if he would have otherwise been selected, that he is not being further considered because a negative result in the drug testing was not obtained.

Do not make further comment or representation. *In particular, do not indicate that the drug(s) involved were illegal or that the applicant is addicted or under the influence.*

Where a business unit offers employment conditional upon completion of drug testing with negative results, applicants should normally not be permitted to begin work. However, if work assignments can not be avoided, an applicant with a positive drug test should be terminated.

Where it is necessary to terminate a newly hired employee because the results of drug testing were positive, the individual should be advised in the limited manner discussed above.

Applicants disqualified because of positive tests should not be reconsidered for employment.

E. DRUG AND ALCOHOL AWARENESS EDUCATION

To assist employees in enhancing their knowledge of alcohol and drug abuse, business units are encouraged to establish educational programs which will broaden employees' knowledge of drug and alcohol abuse and its consequences.

F. IMPLEMENTATION

Implementation and enforcement of policies and practices based on this GUIDE will vary with the type of employee, group and facility involved. For example, plant rules relating to factory employees probably should not contain provisions with respect to business lunches, or the passenger section of aircraft since they are not normally involved in such situations. Similarly, while penalties for violation of plant rules are customarily posted for factory employees, they are not usually posted for salaried employees. They should however, be communicated by appropriate alternate means.

Note: For further information, please contact Dr. John Burns at (612)-670-5102.

PHILIPS INDUSTRIES INC.
ALCOHOL AND DRUG POLICY
November 15, 1986
Corporate Policy and Plant Rules

The Philips Industries alcohol and drug abuse policy comprises a variety of components: a letter to all employees, a corporate policy, and guidelines for supervisors. In addition, all employees are asked to sign a pledge in support of a substance free workplace—a unique approach. The pledge (see page 132) is voluntary, and emphasizes the *entire* company's desire to insure a safe work enviroment.

September 10, 1986

Dear Fellow Employee:

This communication is designed to acknowledge an essential and most important management responsibility we owe each individual employed by Philips Industries. This fundamental obligation is that of providing a productive, safe workplace. For the twenty-nine years of our history, Philips Industries has been committed to this principle. I was recently shocked and appalled to find that many of our work areas are infected with drug and alcohol problems.

Everyone who reads these paragraphs should be aware of the high cost in terms of human suffering, broken families, and untold personal financial burdens that result from alcohol and drug abuse. The national news has been dominated for months by the scope of this problem.

Philips Industries will not tolerate chemical abuse in our workforce and workplace. The cost in human and economic terms dictates that we make every reasonable effort to operate with a chemical free workforce, in a chemical free workplace.

Unfortunately, there exists no simple and quick solution to this problem. However, in the next few weeks, each of you will receive a copy of the Philips Industries Inc. Drug and Alcohol Policy, which will become effective November 15, 1986. The final draft of this important Policy is being reviewed with every effort being made to produce a fair, yet effective tool to combat this major concern. Each of you has the right to expect every management effort to insure that you are not endangered by working alongside the chemically impaired individual.

None of us has the answer to this national tragedy. We *Can* and *Will* make every solemn effort to provide you with a chemical free plant, or office, to perform your tasks.

However, management cannot do it alone. We need your help. We are asking you to sign a pledge to help solve this insidious problem. Together we will succeed.

God bless you all.

Jesse Philips
Founder and Chairman of the Board

PHILIPS INDUSTRIES INC.
ALCOHOL AND DRUG POLICY

I POLICY, PURPOSE AND SCOPE

This Policy is intended as a general statement of Corporate concerns and guide to its intentions regarding alcohol and illegal drug use in the workplace. Specific Policies will be defined, and published by Corporate Personnel and Industrial Relations for use in the Company's manufacturing and warehouse facilities, as well as for those engaged in transportation and non-manufacturing responsibilities.

Both this General Policy and specific policies shall be subject to appropriate periodic revisions consistent with practical considerations and developing legal guidelines.

II DRUG AND ALCOHOL USE ON THE JOB

The use or possession of alcohol, drugs or other intoxicants creates a serious threat to the health and well being of the user along with fellow employees.

The responsibility of Philips Industries is to provide a work environment free of drugs and alcohol. Employees have the right to perform their duties with unimpaired co-workers.

Employees using, selling, transferring or possessing alcohol, or non-prescription drugs on the Company's premises, shall be subject to immediate descipline, following an appropriate investigation and review by Management.

III POLICY GUIDELINES

(A) *Pre-employment Testing*
Consistent with the commitment to provide a drug and alcohol free work environment, Philips Industries Inc., at its discretion, may require job applicants to submit to a pre-employment drug and alcohol screen.
(B) Voluntary testing may be appropriate regarding routine physical examinations, such as annual physicals, return to

work physicals, and other job related circumstances.

(C) Individual testing shall be required when there is reasonable suspicion that drugs or alcohol is affecting job performance and conduct in the workplace.

(D) Any random, or surprise testing on a wholesale basis would be rarely used, and must be preceded by clear evidence of probable abuse by a large number of individuals within the group.

(E) Employees engaged in the operation of vehicles, who as a part of their transportation duties, are required to be physically certified under DOT regulations, shall have an alcohol and controlled substance screen as a mandatory part of such physical examination. A negative result is required as a condition of continued employment.

All individuals to be tested must be advised of the purpose and possible consequences of the particular test. Every effort shall be made to insure confidentiality of test results.

IV DEFINITIONS

Administration—The Corporate Personnel Department is responsible for the content and interpretation of this document, and all questions should be directed to the Personnel Department.

Coverage—All employees, vendors and their employees.

Legal Drug—prescribed drugs and over-the-counter drugs which have been (under U.S. law) legally obtained and are being used for their intended purpose, or as prescribed.

Drug—Any drug which has not been legally obtained or is not being used for its intended purpose or as prescribed. This also includes marijuana.

Under the Influence—The employee is affected by a drug, or alcohol, or both in any detectable manner. The symptoms of influence are not confined to those consistent with misbehavior or to obvious impairment of physical or mental ability, such as slurred speech or difficulty in maintaining balance.

Company Premises—All Company property including vehicles, lockers and parking lots.

Company Property—Includes all Company owned property used by employees such as vehicles, lockers, desks, closets, etc.

Search—Industrial search practices such as inspections of employee personal property including briefcases, lunchboxes or tool-boxes, will be maintained as part of the Company's general security measures. All employees will be expected to cooperate as a condition of employment with special drug/alcohol searches of vehicles, purses, clothing, briefcases, or other employee personal property containers when there is reason to believe that an employee may be in possession of drugs or alcohol. Searches of Company premises and Company property can be conducted at any time.

Clean Test Results—"Clean Test" results are results that indicate no trace of alcohol, or drugs in the employee's system, other than properly used prescription medication.

Testing—Is generally defined as a urine, blood, or breath test to determine chemical or drug content. Testing can occur in the following instances:

(A) Pre-employment process;
(B) Routine physical examination;
(C) Probable and reasonable cause to suspect use;
(D) Mandatory screens for DOT drivers.

Test results will remain confidential.

PHILIPS INDUSTRIES INC.
PLANT RULES AND POLICY
NOVEMBER, 1986

In recognition of the importance, both in human and economic terms, of alcohol and drug abuse in the plant, your Management is committed to make every effort to have a drug and alcohol free workplace and workforce.

The Policy and Rules stated below become effective one month from the date of this Notice.

I (A) The use, consumption, possession, distribution, or sale of illegal drugs and controlled substances and/or unauthorized alcohol while on Company premises is absolutely prohibited. Use of alcohol or illegal drugs prior to reporting for work which results in negative work performance, or erratic conduct in the workplace is likewise prohibited.

Compliance with this prohibition will be strictly enforced. Violations shall result in disciplinary measures as outlined herein.

Compliance with this Policy is a condition of continued employment for all employees.

(B) Employees taking drugs prescribed by an attending physician must advise their direct Supervisor in writing of the possible effects of such medication regarding their job performance and physical/mental capabilities. This written information must be communicated to Management prior to the employee commencing work.

II Managers who have reasonable cause to suspect that an employee has in their possession, or is under the influence of, alcohol or controlled substances, may take the following specific actions:

(A) Possession, sale, distribution, or witnessed use of alcohol or illegal drugs shall result in immediate suspension subject to possible termination of employment, following investigation.

(B) Employees who reasonably appear to be under the influence of alcohol, or controlled substances, shall be subject to immediate suspension, pending investigation, and disciplinary action.

(C) Any available evidence should be collected, i.e., beer cans, liquor bottles.

Under II (B), Disciplinary action shall normally be as follows:

(1) An admisssion by an employee of being under the influence of alcohol, or drugs, shall result in a thirty (30) day suspension and a required "clean" test result for alcohol and drugs. The test shall be administered at the end of the thirty (30) day period and prior to being reinstated. Also, the employee shall be placed on a twelve (12) month probationary period following their

return to work. This provision is available to first time offenders only. Second offenses are covered in 3 (c) below. The employee may be tested at any time during this twelve month period without prior notice.

(2) Employees who deny being under the influence of either alcohol or drugs, shall be given the opportunity to be administered a blood or urine test in support of their denial.

Failure to take such test shall result in a ninety (90) calendar day suspension. In order to be considered for reinstatement, the employee must submit to an appropriate alcohol or drug screen examination· with a negative result.

(3) Employees reasonably suspected of being under the influence, who voluntarily submit to an appropriate test, shall be treated in the following manner:

(A) A negative test conclusion shall result in the employee being immediately returned to work with payment of any loss of wages or benefits suffered during this period of time and interview records will be destroyed.

(B) A positive test result shall result in a thirty (30) day suspension with a "clean test" requirement for reinstatement at the end of the suspension. Also, a twelve (12) month probationary period shall be imposed. A follow-up test can be conducted at anytime during the probationary period.

(C) Employees testing positive for a second time within a twelve (12) month period shall be subject to immediate termination of employment.

(D) Employees disagreeing with test results may choose to have a second set of comparable tests at their expense. In order to be recognized, the laboratory capabilities must be medically recognized and the second test must be performed within six (6) hours of the Company instituted test.

Test results of a significant difference shall allow the reinstatement of such employee if accompanied by medical explanation of differing results. A second incident within twelve (12) months shall result in immediate suspension pending investigation.

(E) Employees attempting to deceive the Company by falsely demonstrating tendencies of being under the influence shall be suspended pending termination. Such suspension shall follow negative test results. Failure to submit to a test in these circumstances shall result in a ninety (90) day suspension. A "clean test" result will be required prior to reinstatement.

III   Employees involved in serious accidents can be required to submit to a urine or blood examination.

IV   Employees requesting aid and guidance from their Management in alcohol and drug abuse resolution will be dealt with on a confidential basis. Help shall be made available without prejudice.

The following section from Philips Industries is included only in the managers' handbook.

PHILIPS INDUSTRIES INC.

POLICIES AND PROCEDURES FOR EMPLOYEES UNDER THE INFLUENCE

This is a Checklist and Procedure for handling employees who are intoxicated or impaired (by legal or illicit drgus).

In order to establish if a violation of Company rules occurred, the following procedure should be followed:

(1) Determine if an employee "appears" to be under the influence of alcohol, drugs, including controlled substances and prescriptions, or both.

(2) Have another Supervisor escort the employee to the Plant Manager's office, along with a lead person if non-union, or if union, have the area Steward involved at the earliest possible point. *Witnesses are critical.* When female employees are involved, at least one other female Supervisor, or lead person should be involved.

(3) Ask the questions contained in the attached "Questions for Suspected Alcohol/Drug Users." A management person should be assigned the task of taking notes of the occurrence including responses to the questions mentioned above.

(4) With everyone present, complete the "Observation Check List."

(5) If the employee agrees, have the employee take the "On-Site Coordination Examination." A refusal will be handled as outlined in Sec. C-2 of the Rules.

(6) Complete the "Opinion Based on Observations" checklist.

(7) If you conclude the employee is not under the influence of drugs/alcohol, and is capable of performing their work duties, return the employee to work.

(8) If the employee is concluded to be under the influence of drugs/alcohol, then suspend them pending final determination, in the presence of the full group, and advise the employee of the rule violated.

(9) Make the necessary arrangements to have the employee taken home. Do not permit the employee to go home or drive alone. If the employee refuses any assistance, such as by his Union Representative, then make sure the Union Representative and your Company Representative *can* verify that the *employee refused such assistance.* However, if an employee cannot control their actions, then under no circumstance should the employee be allowed to leave without assistance. You must call the local police Chief, or Sherrif to warn them of the grievant's condition and refusal of assistance before the employee is allowed to leave the plant. Advise the law enforcement officials of the employee's name and make of car. Advising local law enforcement authorities and pro-

viding assistance before the employee leaves the plant avoids Company liability and limits harm to the employee and other persons.

It is imperative that reliable Management and Employee/Union Representative witnesses be present during all of the above. Appropriate notes and documentation must be preserved for future use. All Management representatives should be familiar with this procedure.

QUESTIONS FOR SUSPECTED SUBSTANCE ABUSERS

1. Are you feeling ill? If yes, What are your symptoms?
2. Are you under a doctor's care? If yes, What are you being treated for? What is your doctor's name and address? When did you last visit the doctor?
3. Are you taking any medication? What medication? Who prescribed? When did you take your last dosage? Do you have your prescription in your possession? Do you have any additional medication in your possession? [Record all information regarding prescription. Request sample, *if permitted* by employee.]
4. Do you have any pre-existing medical problems? Diabetes? Are you taking insulin? Do you have low blood sugar? Epileptic?
5. Do you have a cold? If yes, are you taking any cold pills? Cough medicine? Antihistamines?
6. Are you using any type of drug? If yes, what? When? Where? With whom? How much?
7. Would you submit to a physical examination to include a blood and urinalysis by a medical doctor or hospital so we can be sure that you are in good health and able to safely perform your job? If no, reasons for refusal. A. Check with hospital for satisfactory arrangements. B. GET SIGNED RELEASE STATEMENT by the employee to have the hospital/physician release information to company (See Philips Form for voluntary submission for physical examination and BLOOD and URINALYSIS TEST). If the employee refuses to sign the STATEMENT for voluntary testing, the employee should be told that he is refusing a direct order which consitutes insubordination and that such refusal will be treated as a

131

presumption that the employee is intoxicated or impaired by drugs to the extent of his/her not being able to do their job and the disciplinary provisions of the rules will followed.

8. Would you submit to a basic coordination test?
9. Did you drink alcohol or an alcoholic beverage today? What did you drink? How much? When did you start? When did you stop? Where did you drink? With whom did you drink?

[There follows an Observation Check List for physical appearan and behavior, with space provided for an "opinion base on observation."]

THE PHILIPS INDUSTRIES INC. PLEDGE:

Endorsement in Support of a Drug-Free Philips Industries Inc.

I BELIEVE that employees of Philips Industries Inc. have the right to work in a safe environment free of drugs and alcohol.

THEREFORE, I give my endorsement to the company in its efforts to make Philips Industries free of drug and alcohol abuse.

SIGNED: _____
        (Employee)

        _____
        (Date)